A Complicated

Love

A straight father,
a gay son and lessons
from a road trip

AComplicatedLove.com

Also by the author

Credible—The Six Leadership Conversations

To father and sons,
mothers and daughters,
both gay and straight,
and to all who have a
relationship with a gay person.

May you come out on their behalf.

Published by Possibil.com Inc.
Sayward, Canada

Book and cover design by Dene Rossouw
Editor: Naomi Pauls

AComplicatedLove.com

Henk, Jared, Chad and Brennan, this one's for you.

Contents

A Complicated Love

Preface

When I heard that my 21-year-old son Jared was gay, I was at first shocked, then disappointed. My disappointment stemmed partly from my expectation that all my sons would be straight. It had never really entered my mind that one of my sons would turn out, well, different.

Why had I never thought about it? Probably because at the time it was inconceivable to me that I, a "real man," could father a child who would turn out to be gay.

My disappointment was not with Jared, but with myself. Jared was in South Africa at the time and I was in my new home, Canada.

I started to ask myself what mistakes I could have made in our relationship. Why is Jared gay? What caused him to become gay? Did I inadvertently cause him to become gay? How have I failed him as a father?

Jared and I began to trade e-mails — a few of the more than seventy e-mails are reproduced in this book. I started to read up about homosexuality and learnt that approximately 10 percent of the world's population declare themselves as gay and gay marriages are becoming an accepted norm in many countries.

Yet many gay people continue to live in fear, always in the shadows.

Three years later Jared came to Canada and we went on a road trip through rural Nova Scotia. Our conversations during that trip taught me that my judgments about homosexuality were without foundation and my beliefs were based on myth and superstition, not facts. I learnt a lot about how unquestioned rules in my head influenced the assumptions I had made.

During our discussions, I also realized I had neither sensed nor responded to the unique challenges Jared faced as he was growing up—I was not aware of what he was going through.

During our road trip, I kept asking myself, If I had been there for him as he worked through and came to understand his sexual orientation, would things have turned out differently? Would our relationship be better now?

So what did I learn? I began this book thinking it was our story, Jared's and mine. In reality, it has become my story. To understand and reach into Jared's experience, I first had to look at my own life and examine my own assumptions about homosexuality.

Our road trip conversations are real, not recalled. With this book in mind and Jared's permission, we placed a digital voice recorder between us as we spoke.

In those conversations, we explored fears, taboos and judgments about gay people, so that we might come to a deeper understanding of ourselves and our relationship.

Our conversations were not always easy or painless. On the fourth day of our road trip, we ended up not speaking to each other for a few hours as we each wrestled with our own demons as a result of what we had said and still wanted to say to each another. Were we both enriched by the process? Absolutely!

Join me as I explore coming out as a parent, the influence of religion on my understanding of homosexuality, and how a shift of mind enabled me to become empathic and accepting of people who are gay.

A Complicated Love

Acknowledgements

This book would not have happened without Jared's willingness to talk so openly about his life. There would have been no e-mails, no road trip, no frank discussions and no personal insights.

As much as they revealed about Jared and his experience of being gay, our courageous and frank conversations unravelled my own fears, beliefs and taboos.

The references to Deborah are an acknowledgement of the role that my life partner played as Jared and I were learning to talk to each other. I am indebted to her for her honest critique of the earlier manuscripts. Her suggestions gave depth and substance to this book.

When I use the word "gay," it is mostly in reference to Jared and our discussions about living as a gay man. My hope is that this book will initiate dialogue between gay, lesbian, transgender, bisexual, queer and straight people, as well as those discovering or questioning their orientation.

To my friends and associates who read drafts of this book and gave encouraging advice and feedback, I say a big thank-you: Sharon Habib, Tracey Wimperly, Jack Boomer, Stephen Hammond, Terri Harlow, Christopher Neep, Marie Carlson, Peter Toppings, Mark Knechtel, Matthew Hinton and Cherie MacLeod.

Naomi Pauls, wordsmith and editor, did a wonderful job of challenging and directing my thoughts towards clarity and more concise prose.

To our sons, Henk, Jared, Chad and Brennan, I am in awe of your loyalty towards each other, your wonderful camaraderie when you are together, and your solidarity with Jared, who happens to be gay.

~I~
Reality check

A Complicated Love

~Chapter 1~
The hug

Regrets? Maybe. This is my last night in Cape Town, South
Africa, my home for the last forty-something years. It is
January, a glorious African summer evening.

Tomorrow my wife Deborah and I will be emigrating to Canada. We are
having a final family get-together to say goodbye to our sons, who are
staying behind to finish their university degrees.

The phone rings. "Hey Dad," says Jared, "we'll be there in a little while."
No problem, I say.

I stir the barbecue coals—a ritual I have done countless times under the
vines at the back of our house, in the quiet neighbourhood of
Durbanville. We are surrounded by 400-year-old Cape wine farms, yet
we are within walking distance to some of the finest shopping malls in
the world.

This move to Canada is big. Very big. It's one thing to resign from our
jobs, sell our lovely house and cars. It's another thing entirely to accept
that our four sons have chosen to stay in South Africa.

I remind myself that because of the high crime rate, we are making the
right decision—to exchange family, friends and financial security for
freedom of movement and quality of life in a new country.

I stare at the street light across the road. Its light is reflected in the still waters of our swimming pool. A few moths circle the glass; their flight patterns seem to rise and fall in sync with the chorus of crickets down below.

What do I say to our sons who won't have me around to do the things that fathers do? This is the last evening to have those conversations that I tend to avoid—to say meaningful things like "I love you," and "This is what I'll miss most about you," instead of platitudes like "Hey, leave the girls alone," or "E-mail me," or "I'm only a phone call away."

I am torn between wishing that this evening were already over and hoping it will never end.

The boys arrive. "Sorry we're late," they say. "We had to finish a couple of things."

No problem, I say. The fire is way too hot for the steaks. Grab a beer—they're in the cooler on the deck.

I realize I didn't have to say a thing. The sound of beer cans being opened has already drowned my words. We migrate to the patio around the pool. The boys, dressed in shorts and T-shirts, sit around the edge of the pool, legs in the water.

The patio light shining through the vines, casts abstracts on the water.

"So what have you been doing all day?" Brennan asks.

Packing and repacking, I reply. And sorting out a few last-minute things. We're way over the weight limit.

"Anything you want to get rid of?" asks Jared with a grin. "Laptops, cameras, bottles of wine . . . anything you don't need will find a good home here."

Okay, better keep your cellphones on tomorrow when we're at the airport, I say in jest, so we can call you in case we have to dump some stuff.

"Well," says Chad, "why don't we just weigh your bags tonight and save you the trouble?"

His comment is met by raucous laughter.

We might dump the cat and some underwear, I say, playing along, but no laptop. Sorry.

"You know, Dad," says Henk, "this cat is the fattest cat on the street. Do you think they will let you into Canada with him?"

He's not fat, I protest. He's one of the healthiest cats you'll ever see. I turn my attention to the Cape salmon, seasoned with apricot jam, spices and white wine, cooking slowly in a greased kettle on a bed of herbs and celery.

A while later I overhear the boys pressing their eldest brother for information. What's that? I ask.

"Henk's in love!"

"It's nothing like that," says Henk. "I went for breakfast with a beautiful woman this morning. She's very intelligent."

Chad mimics, "She's very intelligent."

"Shut up, Chad! Her name is Lola. She's a waitress on Kloof Street." Jared steps in. "No, listen, she's really nice. I've worked with her at Waldo's. But she does have a weird in-your-face hairstyle." He catches Chad's eye. Chad sniggers.

Brennan laughs too. "I'll give you a hundred bucks if you call her up right now and tell her to come down here. I want to see this."

I sit back and listen. The evening is getting off to a good start. At moments like this I know I'll miss my guys terribly: their sharp sense of humour and the way they trade puns and fool around and, most of all, their camaraderie.

After tomorrow I won't be around to help when their cars break down, or when they need help moving to a new apartment. I won't be around for our regular Saturday morning breakfasts. I won't be around, period.

As the evening wears on, we trade stories and talk about everything from university degrees to politics to Canadian weather. The more I persuade my sons that Canada is not only Inuit and igloos, the more they remind me that I'll freeze my butt off.

"You'll get cabin fever. You'll get delusional," they say. "And when you do see the sun, you'll bow down and worship it."
They love to tease me. Amidst the laughter, I notice that Jared is unusually quiet.

~::~

Deborah and I love the cosmopolitan lifestyle, the culture and the vibe of Cape Town, one of the most spectacular cities in the world. Apartheid is gone, Nelson Mandela has completed his term of office, and the second democratic elections have taken place, peacefully.

But, alas, the honeymoon is over. People are experiencing an increasing crime rate as the government fails to deliver on its promises of housing, healthcare and providing economic and educational opportunities for disenfranchised members of the population.

The subject of lawlessness and government inefficiencies creep into every conversation—in coffee bars, pubs and restaurants. People are becoming obsessed with their personal security, and this has led to some heated debates in our own family over the past six years, as we've tried to articulate our dilemma—to stay and hope the situation improves or start from scratch in a new country.

The boys want to finish their schooling and degrees and then they will decide where they want to live, be it South Africa, the United Kingdom, Canada or wherever. They have a different perspective on the future of their country and want to stay with their friends, at least for now.

We know that in a few years, we will not be eligible to emigrate because our ages will count against us. Already many in South Africa are living in gated communities and behind security fences. I came across an Interpol report indicating that South Africa had the highest murder rate of the countries selected, with 59 murders per 100,000 people compared to six murders per 100,000 in the USA. If we are living under siege now, how will it be in twenty years' time?

It is past midnight. I throw a few pieces of wood on the fire and stoke the coals. We gather round as we sip Amarula, a sweet liqueur made from a wild African fruit.

Jared disappears and returns with a package neatly wrapped in brown paper and tied with string.

"It's from all of us," says Jared, "but you have to open it on the plane." We thank the boys. I sense that this is not a gift that money can buy.

The time has come to say goodbye. We had agreed that none of the boys would come to the airport tomorrow. I have steeled myself for this moment. I feel a stab of anguish. A haunting memory flashes through my brain. More than ten years ago, their mother and I took the boys for a drive. I parked the car and explained to the boys, who were then small enough to sit together on the back seat of the car, that their mother and I were going to separate.

Your mom and I are going to live apart for a while, I said to their watchful, innocent faces. I am going to move out and live in another house nearby.

"But Dad," said Jared, then only ten years old, "when will we see you?" Everything will be nearly the same as it's always been, except that I will come and see you guys often, and you will come and stay over at my place, I said, not knowing the implications of my words.

I can't forget the look on their faces. What feelings were imprinted on their psyches? Was it a sense of betrayal, abandonment?

Now, years later, I'm happily remarried. The boys are very comfortable around Deborah, but I know Jared is highly intuitive and senses things. What do he and his brothers really think about us going away? Does it make them feel insecure? Are they angry with us for abandoning them? We wander out from the house to the drive.

I love you guys, I hear myself say. I'm going to miss you.
I give each of my boys a hug. Jared is last. When we hug, Jared holds on much longer than the others.

When the tail lights of his VW beetle fade into the long summer night, I walk slowly back to the house and stop at the edge of the pool. My eyes well up. I remove my clothes and slip into the cool, turquoise water.

~::~

The next day dawns clear. Not a cloud in sight. If the prevailing summer southeast wind is blowing, pilots flying out from Cape Town International usually head due south over the sea before turning north to Johannesburg or Europe.

Today is different. The pilot doesn't try to reach maximum altitude right away but flies at about 2,000 metres in a southwesterly direction over the sea. When we reach the long spike of land that divides the Indian and Atlantic oceans, the jet banks over in a slow arc towards the Atlantic. As we set a slow northerly course just above the Twelve Apostles, I see the view our pilot intended.

Arsonists have set fire to the magnificent mountains of the Cape of Storms, home to one of the most diverse floral kingdoms on earth. As we approach Table Mountain, I see more fires ravaging the mountainside.

Through the smoke I recognize many of the nooks, crannies and peaks that I've explored over the years. I am glued to the tiny window. Happy memories of endless days on these mountains surface within me. I don't want to see this unnecessary wanton destruction, but I continue to crane my neck as we slowly pass the landmarks I know so well.

As the smoke and fires start to recede in the distance, I notice the passengers have become silent.

After a while I reach into my hand luggage for the gift wrapped in brown paper. A small handmade book is tucked beneath some tissue. I open the cover. On each page is a handwritten message from my sons, family members and close friends.

Now I know why Jared called to say they were going to be late. He was collecting farewell messages and binding the book.

I nudge Deborah and read a message from each of our boys. The last page is from Jared.

> *Dear Dad,*
> *I meant to write this earlier and I am still thinking of what to say on the very eve of your leaving. You must admit that we've always been late one way or another.*
> *I'm positive about the move and realize now that we must all truly follow our dreams. If there is one life principle I'd like to live by, this would be it!*
> *This move will open more opportunities for us all and will broaden all of our horizons. We have no mandate on the past, yet I do look back with good memories. So many people look up to and admire you and I've become one of them.*
> *Thank you for what you've done the past few years.*
> *Love, Jared*

Although Jared's letter appears upbeat and positive,
I know he has deep feelings about my moving away. I sensed it when we hugged last night.

I stare out the window, overwhelmed by this parting gift.

A Complicated Love

~Chapter 2~
Digging deep

A year and a half later. We're living in Nova Scotia, Canada, two minutes from the sea on St. Margaret's Bay, just west of Halifax. With the longer days and warmer nights of July upon us, I reflect on our move from Cape Town.

Our new house is surrounded by trees and freshwater lakes. We have been embraced by the local community and relish their hospitality, the open spaces, the bay with its many idyllic coves and islands, and the fact that our doors are seldom locked.

I receive an e-mail from Carol, Jared's mother, a few days before his twenty-first birthday. "Jared is going to call you. I think he's got something really important to say."

I read those words a few times. If Jared needs help with something, I realize I can't do much because I am in Canada and he is in South Africa.

Is he changing direction at university? Is he going to quit university and get a job? Is he planning to travel through Africa again, like he did before?

Although fathers are often blamed for being totally out of touch, I know it is none of these.

The day before his birthday, Deborah, intuitively says, "Do you recall that whenever Jared invited friends to stay over, we've never seen him with a girlfriend?"

She has mentioned this before and I have always responded with comments like "He's a popular guy," and "He's in no hurry to get serious with a girl."

I learn later that she sensed Jared was about to tell me something that would change my relationship with him forever.

~::~

During Jared's high school years, he had had many girlfriends but never seemed attracted to any particular girl. As I wait for his call, I mull over what Deborah was hinting at.

I remember watching Jared one year in a school play. He's always been an outstanding actor, but his acting that year had seemed to emphasize behaviours and gestures I had not seen him use before. His posturing seemed so out of character and made me feel so uncomfortable that I had spoken to him about it afterwards. I remember telling him to cut out effeminate behaviours because he wasn't a girl and that people would laugh at him.

During that time, when Jared came over to stay on his weekends with me, I remember he spent a lot of time helping out and cooking in the kitchen with Deborah.

What can be so important that Carol would e-mail me to give me a heads-up? Although still in denial, I think that on the off-chance that Jared is going to tell me he is gay, I have a lot of questions.

First, I want to know whether I am to blame in some way. And why would Jared decide to come out now, at twenty-one years of age? If Jared is gay, how should I relate to him from now on?

Then Jared calls.

As I hear his voice, my mind goes into a spin. Should I engage him in perfunctory conversation like Hi Jared. How're you doing? So what's new in your part of the world? Or What's the latest on your bursary? Or should I make it easier for him by saying, Jared, I heard from your mom that you have something to tell me . . .

Instead, Jared takes the initiative. "Dad, I need to tell you something," he says. "You probably have an idea, but I need to tell you that I've come out and I need you to know that I'm gay."

Should I say, *Well done, Jared, that took courage*? I try to keep my voice as normal as possible so as not to let Jared know that mixed emotions are welling up inside me. I say something like, *Your mom gave me a heads-up and I want you to know it's okay with me, Jared. I'm not going to treat you any different than before.*

What I really want to ask is, Jared, after twenty-one years, how do you know that you're gay? But I don't. And somehow the conversation ends. A bunch of questions floods my mind. Why do I feel a sense of dread?

Why do I fear he has been lost to the other side? Why do I question whether I have failed as a father and a role model? Is part of my reaction rooted in my religious programming about gays? And how will I react when Jared wants to bring his boyfriend over to stay for the holidays?

I secretly hope Jared is going through a phase. What if I can persuade him to reconsider his "choice" of lifestyle because he has the potential to become "normal" again?

I think about being a weekend dad during Jared's teenage years. We spent time together going on hikes, we had Saturday morning breakfasts together, we spoke about stuff. During those times, I never questioned why he hadn't gotten serious with girls.

A feeling of angst descends upon me. Had I found it easier to hide behind bravado, rather than sensing and responding to the unique challenges Jared was facing?

When I left school, I was determined to prove I was a tough guy, so I joined the paratroopers in South Africa. The training at No. 1 Parachute Battalion made me extremely fit and mentally resilient. After military service, I became a preacher and worked primarily with biker groups.

I recall we had only two rules to encourage bikers to join our breakfast runs and biker rallies: *Come as you are* and *We never cancel.*

The second rule earned me and my team great respect amongst the biker community because we rode big bikes and we rode in any weather.

We never cancelled.

The first rule is the one that bothers me though. Part of my strategy as a preacher was to play pool with bikers in pubs on Friday and Saturday nights.

Once I and my team had built up relationships with individual bikers, we would invite them to join us on our regular breakfast runs on Sunday mornings. Most times I would be the speaker. My acceptance of bikers as they were and meeting them on their own turf contributed to the success of those events over a period of ten years.

What concerns me is my double standard. I was totally accepting of a biker lifestyle. I always met with bikers on their turf. Yet I was unwilling, when Jared was growing up, to entertain the thought that he might be gay and if so, to really engage with him. I never took the time to meet him on his turf.

Had I been in denial and unconsciously opted for a conspiracy of silence rather than engaging him? Was this because I had a stereotypical image of gay male traits in my mind?

In retrospect, I was probably more comfortable avoiding talking about any of Jared's behaviours that triggered the stereotype in my mind. In the ritual of pleasantries, had I insulated myself from looking into Jared's eyes, so that I wouldn't have to confront the taboos lurking in my head?

If I had really listened to him, could I have been there for him as he worked through and came to understand his sexual orientation?

Was my avoidance of sexuality and possible awkward discussions deliberate, because I interpreted self-disclosure as mushy weakness? After that telephone call, aside from the occasional e-mail and perfunctory phone call, we don't communicate very much. More accurately, I don't communicate much. Instead, I retreat into a cocoon and reflect on my role as a father.

~::~

I rack my brains to find the source of my homophobia. Clearly it wasn't my friendship with Bill Broadbent, my best buddy during my early teens. We were very close, so close in fact that we both used his bed at the same time to make 'love' to our girlfriends. I was paired up with his sister and Bill with his sister's friend.

On another occasion, propped naked on smooth rocks inside a mountain cave overlooking the city, we held a masturbation competition. A small waterfall cascaded over the mouth of the cave, forming a curtain between us and the hum of societal norms in the city far below.

Our relationship was very much like David and Jonathan of the Old Testament—we wrestled, practiced judo moves on each other, hiked mountains, did many crazy things and tried to make out with girls together.

I do remember explaining to another friend how to masturbate. I don't recall how the conversation came up, but I'm sure it was pretty brief and matter of fact.

He had no clue that his body could experience such wonderful feelings. Two experiences that could have planted seeds of homophobia come to mind.

I remember cycling with Bill one time on a mountain road overlooking the city. I was about 14 years old at the time. While we admired the view after a bit of a climb, a man approached us and offered as drinks from a cooler in the trunk of his car. We both accepted the drinks. I remember him asking where we were going and we pointed to Signal Hill, which was about ten kilometres away.

He said he was also going to Signal Hill and we were welcome to have another drink when we got there. When we got close to the end of the road at Signal Hill, I saw his car pulled over up ahead with the trunk open. I rode up ahead of Bill.

As I drew up next to the driver's side, I turned to thank the man before taking a drink. To my shock and surprise, he was playing with himself.

I spun my bike round and shouted to Bill as he rode up, "Homo, get out of here, he's a homo, get out of here!"

We sped off as fast as we could.

Both Bill and I were Sea Scouts at the time and the second instance happened about a year later while we were both working on a small sailboat down at the Royal Cape yacht club.

As we worked weekends trying to get our sailboat into shape for sailing in the harbour, a man called Mr. Hawkins, who was working on his own sailboat, would come over and offer us advice and the odd spare part or two.

He soon discovered we lived pretty close to where he lived and so he would offer us a ride home at the end of each day.

Sometimes Hawkins would drop Bill off at his home first and then drop me off. On other occasions, Hawkins would drop me off first and then take Bill home.

When I was alone with Hawkins in his car, he would show me pornographic photographs and advise me on the best ways to masturbate using various household oils and creams.

When I told Bill what Hawkins was doing, he said that Hawkins was doing the same with him.

From that moment on, every time we walked past Hawkins' house at night, we threw stones on his roof and shouted at the top of our voices, so the neighbours could hear, "Hawkins is a homo, Hawkins is a homo!"

We never saw Hawkins again.

It's possible these two experiences plus the homophobic culture of my army days, combined with my own religious acculturation during seventeen years as a church minister in South Africa contributed to my narrow understanding of human sexuality.

Working with bikers, ex-convicts and youth, I was convinced that when it came to issues like homosexuality, the Bible was clear in its condemnation.

To "protect" the people in my care and prevent them from going astray, my point of view was God's point of view, which was the only point of view. My lack of empathy for gays and outright rejection of homosexuality reflected my shallow understanding of the real issues.

Maybe Jared gave signals that he was discovering his sexual orientation. Had I deflected them away from my emotional radar? Did he pick up signs from me that homosexuality was unacceptable?

A few months pass. Then one day, I see an e-mail with "Hi" in the subject line. It's from Jared.

> *Dad, Hi! How are you today?*
> *You have been very silent. Is this because you are busy, or because you are not keen to write back?*
>
> *Why is it that I have to milk information from you? And why is it that I don't give up information freely to you? I wrote a letter at the beginning of the term and asked you some questions.*

It's not a big thing, but I wonder why you don't reply. When you do, then I still have to milk information out of you.

I am going to see a therapist this coming week.
Jared

I leave the e-mail for a few days with every intention of getting back to Jared.

To my dismay, I realize I have ignored his earlier e-mail because his questions about our past got at the very core of who I was as a father and my relationship with him. I didn't want to go there.

Even though I can make an excuse and say we were moving house at the time, it's not the real reason for my not replying sooner.

It comes as a surprise that Jared is going to see a therapist. I had no idea that he is working through issues and that he needs the help of a professional to work through them.

I reflect again on how I might have contributed to his state of mind. I am so far removed from his world, emotionally and geographically, I have no idea what he is going through. I send off a reply, hoping that I can offer a few answers and an apology.

Hey Jared,
Sorry for my late reply. We have just bought a house and I was busy with the move. I realize that as you read this, you might think I'm hiding behind excuses. To be honest, I am.

I filed your e-mail away, hoping to reply to you soon, when in fact I was dragging my heels because your questions made me look inside myself and I didn't want to go there. Okay, now I've got that off my chest.

I know I wasn't around for much of the time when you needed me. Although we did do quite a lot of things together such as mountain hikes, I wish I had been more available to you. My years as a church minister took their toll. People were in and out of our house all the time. It was like living in a bus shelter. In the end, it so affected my relationship with your mom that we split up.

While I licked my wounds, I began to see an old school friend. After a time, I realized the relationship was going nowhere. One of the reasons I decided to end the relationship was because I used up so much emotional energy keeping the relationship on track that I had nothing left to provide you guys with the emotional closeness and protection you deserved. So after some hard thinking and inner turmoil, I broke off the relationship and moved out.

At that stage I had to repay the bank a 100k loan for my business that had collapsed. My focus at the time was on trying to survive emotionally, and I paid insufficient attention to you guys and the business. Looking back now, I realize that when one goes through a divorce, one's ability to cope is extremely compromised.

Mine certainly was. It was not an easy experience to go through because my whole life was destabilized. I had to sell our house, pay maintenance for you guys and learn to survive from day to day and paycheque to paycheque.

I hated owing money. So, I made a decision to pay back the loan and get out of the hole I had dug for myself.

Luckily I had a good 8 to 5 job, so I started moonlighting after hours teaching guitar, writing scripts, producing videos and providing skills training to private companies. But even though I worked 16-hour days during those first few years, I just managed to keep my head above water. That's why you never saw me. I was in survival mode. It was either swim or sink.

I started to date Deborah. And from then on things improved. We complemented each other. She was a great help in getting me back on the road — we've been together 12 years now. Looking back now I realize that for those years when you needed me most I was not around.

Unfortunately, you and the boys got caught in the middle of me trying to sort out my life. I have no idea how this affected you and I would like to talk about that some day. I hope this explains some things.
Love, Dad

A few days later I receive a long response from Jared. I am amazed at his insight and his maturity as he's worked through issues and gone to therapy. I regret we never had conversations like this face to face.

Hey Dad,

Thank you for this last letter. It really means a lot to me.

I'd really like to work some more on this, and it really helps when you can reply and answer some of my questions.

I have never had a long-term relationship and this really grates me. Part of this is my sexuality, but there are much deeper themes at play here.

Relationships are a big problem area for me, with friends and with potential boyfriends. The fact of the matter is that I am extremely good socially, I know how to speak and behave. I'm a good social chameleon and I play by the rules. I have lots of friends as well.

But this doesn't hide the fact that I'm not very happy in many of my relationships, and most of them are not on the level that I would wish them to be.

At the root of all my social relationships is a deep and extremely powerful feeling of unworthiness. It is this "driver" that powers so many of my interactions and manifests itself cruelly in many other things I think about.

Consequently, somehow I've picked up a need to make myself special, to stand out from the crowd and be original. In my teens, this has been very powerful, this feeling that the only way I can be worthy is by putting myself into a position where I can be special and different.

I have become especially good at making myself different, or convincing myself that I am different. This is my defence.

At the same time, I have had an incredibly strong need to just be one amongst the crowd. To be accepted. So on one hand I put myself into superior positions and on the other, all I want to do is join everybody else.

I must always be the main actor on the stage, push myself into the limelight. I must win everybody's approval and will put myself through whatever it takes to get the approval I need.

So when it comes to relationships, I have gotten into the habit of arranging everybody I meet into two categories. Either they are boring and normal and consequently not worth my attention because I feel superior. Or they are my superiors, people I want to be like and to emulate. I guess a lot of this is natural. But with me there is an inherent judgment.

When someone is simply different, I construe it as better or worse. This kind of thinking has manifested itself especially in the few infatuations that I have had.

The trend here is that I fall head over heels and extremely destructively in love with other boys firstly who are very like me and secondly whom I have no chance with, often straight men.

From the very beginning I know that my fantasies will never happen, so I can dream and dream them. In this sense, I can project all my own wishes and desires onto other people, in the vain hope that they will turn around and rescue me.

Thus, I can dream and at the same time maintain the feeling that I am a victim and that I am just waiting for the right person to recognize all my good qualities.

I stop reading to wonder where Jared's feeling of unworthiness comes from. Has my search for identity and a place in the world been transferred to him via emotional osmosis? And in trying to connect and find an anchor for his life, did he inadvertently cling to an aspect of me that I would have preferred he had not seen?

His e-mail shows he's doing a lot of self-reflection as he's working through issues and going to therapy. I admire his insight and at the same time I feel a sense of loss because I could have engaged him at a deeper level when we were together. In the swirl of busyness, I missed some vital cues and opportunities.

After his mom and I separated, she downloaded emotionally on the boys over a period of years.

It was her way of clearing her emotions about me and our relationship that wasn't working as she tried to gain a sense of self in the turmoil after our divorce.

I sensed this during the time because Jared, and indeed all the boys, were very supportive of her, to the point that I felt a distance from them, almost as if I had betrayed them when I sought a way out of the emotional impasse.

Although she now regrets she painted such a bleak picture of me, Jared, who seemed more vulnerable and sensitive to negative emotions than his brothers at the time, must have tried to protect her from the emotional roller coaster that divorce brings, and formulated a largely negative perception of me.

My absence, his negative perception of me, and living with a single mom must have all had a tremendous influence on his sense of self during his formative years.

I regret I never knew that Jared was so self-aware and able to articulate and disclose his innermost thoughts and feelings.

Having grown up watching movies where the norm was to feature the hero as a white male with a stunted vocabulary, I had always interpreted self-disclosure as a sign of femininity or weakness. I now realize it's a sign of strength.

I continue reading Jared's e-mail in which he shares his relationship frustrations:

In this sense I fall in love with men in whom I recognize myself. It's like Narcissus with the pond that reflects himself.

I see qualities that I recognize in myself in this person. And I project them on to that person strongly, so that eventually that is all I can see.

I convince myself that this is what I want. When actually, what I really want is for that person to somehow bring out those qualities in me.

I'm like a moth to a lamp. I'm hoping — oh so hoping — that this person will bring me out.

In fact, the men I fall in love with are those people that come close to my ideal partner. And what I've discovered is that that ideal partner is in fact me. But it is the me that I want to be so badly.

So I am waiting for myself, for that prince, who is never going to come.

And so the people who I admire the most are those in whom I recognize myself. But I refuse to acknowledge this and end up competing with them for attention, to prove to myself that I am better and do embody these mysterious qualities. I am in continuous competition with others.

But always, always, always I feel like the dog. I am the person who is never myself, who can't be because he is always trying to be someone else—better, more special.

And pervading all of this is a habitual horrible thought pattern that is so negative and extremely destructive. It knocks me down again and again. And I always rise up for more because I think I deserve it. I know I can do better.

All in all I lack this feeling of worthiness. And this is what I am and have to work on. I need to try to reclaim a sense of self-worth.
And I need to concentrate on how I feel and listen to my true self. For so long I have been trying to be this projected person. Believing that I can be me, then I can just be.

If I can make space for myself and be easier on myself, then I am sure that I will discover that I am in fact the person that I've always thought I was. Not the person that I am always running away from or trying to be. Travelling up Africa. Busy, busy, busy. Running, running, running.

I might be pleasantly surprised by who I find. But the important thing is to look inward and not outward or upwards.

So Dad, I guess what I really need from you is to help me try to find out where I picked up this feeling of unworthiness.

I am interested in the divorce years because they were so especially traumatic and we all got hurt really badly.

But in my mind, this period was really just a development on what had already been laid. I want to know more about our home when I was a little kid . . .

I have never disclosed to Jared one of the main reasons why I eventually left his mother when our boys were growing up. I had a very successful church ministry to bikers, and our house had become a refuge for the needy. My attention was all over the place rather than at home.

Over the next few years, his mom, feeling excluded and lonely, had a few infatuations and an affair with one of my good friends. When I discovered what was going on, it hit me so hard I felt I was having a heart attack. From that moment on, things were never the same again between the two of us.

I reluctantly went for some counselling with colleagues, but to no avail. My trust was broken, my pride was crushed and my heart was numb.

Two years later, after the marriage had broken up, I sensed I was about to go through a similar wrenching break-up again with a girlfriend.

I wrote a series of morbid love songs reflecting my frame of mind, in an attempt to express my feelings. Buried amongst all my guitar music, I find the one called "Shadowlands."

As you went out the door
I knew I'd been here before
I couldn't stop the shaking
As my heart was breaking
From the look in your eye
I knew it was your goodbye
I was hurting pretty deep
Why was I feeling so cheap?

So, I guess working through my issues and being emotionally absent from Jared during his formative years meant his need for a real connection with me could never have been fully met. His e-mail concludes:

Last night I went to see some jazz dancing. One of the jazz art performers did a dance with his young nephew who was only six or so.

This really touched me deeply, because the man and the boy danced so beautifully. Something about the way the uncle touched and held his nephew and moved him around.

This is the feeling I am working with. There is a root in me that is missing the message: You are okay just the way you are.

And I feel that when I was younger I somehow never got that. Love, Jared.

After a week of soul-searching, I feel ready to reply to Jared. Rekindling painful memories and telling him about myself is not easy for me.

How often have I looked the other way or moved the conversation to safer ground?

There were many times as a family, I felt it was better to say nothing, so as not to provide fodder for his mom, who in the likeness of her own mother, was prone to indulge in gargantuan tantrums over the smallest things.

I realize now that my response was an escape, a habit so entrenched that when I tuned out and got lost in my own thoughts, my disconnectedness only made things worse.

After rationalizing about my reasons for avoiding open conflict and thorny issues, I decide to start writing the e-mail anyway, hoping my jumbled thoughts will make sense as I go along.

> *Dear Jared,*
> *Thanks for your e-mail. The insights you shared about yourself have triggered a great deal of introspection for me. I hope that what I am about to tell you will give both of us some clarity on where I am coming from and what we can learn from it.*
>
> *Perhaps the best way I can start this journey is by telling you about my own childhood.*
>
> *No early memories or experiences stand out for me. It's pretty much a blank. As a kid I never once went hiking, fishing or camping with my father.*

I now know my father was going through his own struggles of self-identity and thus never connected with me in those early years at all. My sense is that those lost opportunities for authentic connection contributed to my low self-image and sense of unworthiness as a gangly youngster. I sense there's a similarity here between my experience of being emotionally disconnected from my father and a possible disconnect between me and you.

As I struggled to find my place in the world, I remember one thing; I felt very alone. I had no friends.

My first few friendships only came about in grade six. After high school I volunteered for the paratroopers. In retrospect, I know I wanted to prove to myself I could persevere despite all types of odds.

Although it was a tough year, getting my wings was a tremendous boost for my confidence and helped to drive away my sense of unworthiness. On weekends off from the military, I remember going for a beer or two with my father to the local pub. It was his way of saying he was proud of me.

My father loved my mother, but in a controlling type of way. He never encouraged her to drive. This limited her potential because she was always dependent on him.

She had this unconditional acceptance of me whatever I did and was a very loving mother and a good example for me.

So the point of this is to say that I was influenced by my parents' relationship. It was a loving relationship yet with no real demonstrations of love, and to varying degrees, throughout my life, I have had to deal with my own yearning to be included and connected.

I now understand that a lack of emotional connection with my father led to my feelings of unworthiness.

Your life and mine seem similar in many respects.

Your e-mail evoked many days of self-reflection because it triggered emotions within me that I never knew were there.

It was especially painful to go back and explore my own need for connection and to come to the conclusion that I would never bring these yearnings to resolution because my parents are no longer alive.

It makes me really value what we are learning about each other.

I still struggle with some issues of unworthiness. I am getting better at dealing with it because I can replace those feelings with a breadcrumb trail of successes that give me perspective and a confidence boost when I need it.

Jared, you mentioned that you tend to be a social chameleon, the main actor on the stage as a way of winning approval.

You also said in your e-mail that you convince yourself that you are different.

My understanding from reading on this topic, in order to sort out my own life, is that we can appear to project an image of a false self in order to please others.

You mentioned you desperately want someone to draw you out and discover your true self. Do you fear that if a lover draws you out, he might back off when he discovers your true self? If so, is that why you have never had a long-term relationship, because you extinguish it before it ignites, to avoid an anticipated rejection?

I'm inquiring because I'm aware that I face this dilemma from time to time. How do I deal with the tension caused by destructive self-talk such as 'I'm not worthy,' and the urge to break out of this cycle and reveal my true self as an authentic human being?

I have recently been reading the work of Harville Hendrix. One of the main premises of his work is the theory of the imago match.

In a nutshell, the imago match has its roots in our early experiences as a helpless child. When we were very young most of us experienced various forms of separation from our caregivers.

Even though the separations could have been part of normal growing up, the sense of disconnect from a loving caregiver is never forgotten and is stored in our memory.

As adults, we are driven to find the original wholeness and connection we once had. Our unconscious brain wants to continue where we left off as a child and wants to connect with our caregivers to complete unfinished conversations and achieve a sense of wholeness and reconnection.

Why did the jazz art dance between the young boy and his uncle touch you so deeply? What did the relationship between the boy and his uncle trigger in you? Did the dance have a subtle sexual connection? Or was it a faint memory of a paradise lost, a reminder of a deep intuitive connection or intimacy the two of us could have experienced?

Hendrix says people transfer their feelings about their parents and caregivers onto their love partners. Through a process of unconscious selection, they choose partners who manifest the familiar good and bad behaviours, mannerisms and habits of their caregivers.

So when we are looking for a partner, our brain scans every person we meet for a possible match. When there's a match, we experience a surge of interest. If there's a near-perfect match, we feel romantically attracted to the other person.

If we fall in "love" with this person, we are in fact in love with an image projected upon that person. Our brain believes it has found the imago match. Our imago in this case is an integrated image of all of our early caregivers and influencers. Our lover complements our weaknesses and reflects who we want to be as a complete person.

And hopefully, our lover will continue the unfinished conversations we never had with our caregivers and satisfy our unconscious need for the connection we experienced in childhood.
So, apart from an imago match that is driven by a need for connection, we are in love with the idea of wish fulfillment.

This is similar but different from Narcissus: we fall in love not with a reflected part of our ideal self, but with a projected image from the past.

This made a lot of sense to me when I thought about my reasons for choosing Deborah as my life partner. It has helped me to understand that a lot of her qualities are a composite of my parents and my aunt, but especially my mother.

As a result, I have become aware of not falling into the trap of only validating those aspects of her personality and her qualities that resonate with the imago embedded in my unconscious.

Apart from having qualities that do match up, I recognize that Deborah is her own person, independent and beautiful. She is not interested in living up to a composite from my past or being constricted by a fantasy of my mind.

The more I resist any attempts by my unconscious to hijack the situation, the more attractive she becomes to me.

Interesting stuff. What do you think?
Love, Dad

After I have sent off the e-mail to Jared, my mind keeps going back to the image of the young boy dancing with his uncle. Jared seemed to be struck by the way the uncle touched his nephew and the way his nephew responded.

When I grew up, touching and hugging were not the norm. I don't recall my father hugging me. The closest I got to a hug was a handshake on my birthday each year, and that was it. I rack my brain to see if I can replay a memory of me embracing or hugging my guys.

When they were younger, we wrestled, playing piggyback and tickling games typical of the roughhousing that most fathers do with their children.

The only time I can recall hugging each of them was when we said our goodbyes as Deborah and I were leaving South Africa for Canada. This speaks volumes about the kind of father I was to them and the oceans that separate us now.

How would my relationship with my sons be different if I had gone beyond the normal games and developed a habit of embracing them, if for no other reason than to acknowledge who they were and what they meant to me?

I'll never know, other than to recognize that when Jared saw the little boy dancing with his uncle, it must have triggered a yearning for a father connection deep within him. If that's true, it was something he never had with me.

I must have been blind to opportunities for a real connection with Jared, partly because my fear for emotional closeness was reinforced by my own conditioning of how a father-son relationship should be.

I cannot recall ever seeing my father hug my mother. My year in the military as a paratrooper obliterated any idea that self-disclosure and intimacy, between a man and another man or between two women, or even between a man and a woman, was okay.

The rules in my head went something like this: Be a man of few words. Never express true feelings (it's a sign of weakness). Hide all signs of vulnerability. Regard any hint of emotional closeness with suspicion.

A week went by. Then Jared sent a short reply.

> *Hey Dad,*
> *What you say about projecting onto others is something I have been thinking about because I catch myself doing it from time to time.*

I'm not so sure I agree on the connection between one's parents and those you fall in love with. I'll have to think about this one a bit more.

I know that every single guy that I've been crazy over is someone whom I would like to be in some way. Perhaps that "in love" feeling is closer to jealousy, a kind of neediness.

Next time I feel this kind of thing I'm going to be a bit more wary.

I'm sure that the real love thing is a bit more subtle and gentle, with less urgency and more time to relax and be myself.

More than likely, I need to learn to open myself to things and have fewer expectations.
Love, Jared

Jared's e-mails get me thinking about how, in subtle ways, I could have sent him messages that I only accepted and approved of a part of him.

When I saw him acting effeminately onstage in the school play, did I somehow let him know that he didn't add up to my mental model of a good and perfect son?

Did fear drive me to unconsciously pressure him to repress part of his true self? If I inadvertently tried to influence him to deny his orientation, could this have resulted in him feeling less whole?

Although I have had low self-esteem from time to time and carried a fair share of "unworthy" baggage, the hardest part of personal growth and self-knowledge for me was the realization that no one could help me regain my self-esteem and feeling of well-being.

This provoked a healthy realism within me. I needed to cross the bridge to authenticity alone.

In my relationship with Deborah, I have never felt I needed to sacrifice my individuality to enhance our relationship. Deborah complements me, but she never rescues me.

If one of us is looking to the other for completeness and fulfillment, or if one of us is more emotionally invested than the other, our relationship comes under strain.

What concerns me about Jared is that he seems to be waiting for a knight on a white horse who will bring him into full bloom and draw him out. I'm concerned that when he thinks this way, he represses his self-worth and well-being in order to please and be accepted by another.

A year goes by. Jared is teaching English in Taiwan. Deborah and I have established a consulting business in Halifax aimed at improving leadership and employee engagement.

Apart from regular calls and e-mails from Jared about day-to-day events, our communication on mutual self-disclosure has dried up. My chief interest is to see whether I played a role in creating the sense of unworthiness that drives him to seek relationships with certain guys.

Clearly this is no different from many heterosexual relationships.
I send off an e-mail hoping I can find some answers.

> *Hey Jared,*
>
> *Way back before you moved to Taiwan, you spoke about your
> sense of unworthiness. You mentioned "I'm like a moth to a
> lamp. I'm hoping — oh so hoping — that this person will bring
> me out." I've been giving a lot of thought to what this means.*
>
> *It worries me that your approach to relationships suggests
> that you are less worthy than your partner and that only
> another person can bring you to full bloom.*
>
> *Think back to your childhood, to when we were all together as
> a family. Where do your feelings of unworthiness come from?
> What role did I have in this? I acknowledge that my need to
> know could be driven by a sense of guilt.*
>
> *I have been soul-searching to see if I unintentionally sent you
> messages urging you to deny your emerging gay orientation.
> Or did I accept only a part of you, the straight part?*
>
> *Did I make you feel less whole because I might have
> inadvertently caused you to repress an essential part of who
> you are?*
>
> *I know these are heavy questions. Please don't think you will
> hurt my feelings. I really need to know.*
> *Love, Dad*

It's now three months since I sent that e-mail. I have had other e-mails from Jared but nothing about unworthiness.

Maybe he sensed my motive was really to learn more about my own shortcomings and he didn't want to hurt me or get into blame mode. I try to imagine how I would feel if my father asked me the same questions.

It would be very difficult for me to arrive at an answer and then disclose it to my father. I guess I'll leave these questions for a more opportune time, when we can speak in person.

~II~

Road trip conversations

A Complicated Love

~Chapter 3~
Arrival

I t is time. Jared's year of teaching English in Taiwan is fast coming
to a close and he will be heading to the U.K. to become a
schoolteacher. I last saw him when I went back to South Africa just
after he had come out as a gay person.

Lately, we have been talking about him visiting me in Canada and going
on a road trip together around Nova Scotia and Cape Breton. We set a
date for October.

He's had a boyfriend and several lovers already. I'm sure he's been
wondering whether I was going to keep him at a safe distance or just
slowly freeze him out. What will it be like to talk face to face after so
long? I'm not sure about my own feelings.

Even though we've had some very open conversations via e-mail and on
the telephone, my heart tells me I have failed him as a father.

Our meaningful conversations have now dried up. How do I broach a
discussion about our relationship without driving a wedge between us?
How do I overcome my own feelings of inadequacy?

How do I recreate a relationship that meets his longing for connection,
acceptance and feeling special? How do I acknowledge my shortcomings
while reminding Jared that we are both ultimately responsible for our
own destinies?

Lastly, how do we interrupt and replace our limiting beliefs about our past and each other with new, authentic experiences?

It is 11 o'clock. I am pacing expectantly in the waiting area of the ferry terminal in Yarmouth, Nova Scotia. The Cat, also known as one of the world's "super ships," takes about three hours to travel from Bar Harbor, on the coast of Maine in the U.S., to Yarmouth.

I lean forward to ask an attendant if the Cat is on time. Just as she is about to answer, I see Jared out of the corner of my eye, coming through the turnstiles.

We hug. Jared is wearing tight-fitting jeans and a blue T-shirt. His hair is trimmed very short. He's looking lean, relaxed and different in the sense that I have not seen him for three years.

After loading his one very large bag into the jeep, we leave Yarmouth for our home on St. Margaret's Bay, near Halifax.

How was the ferry ride? I ask as we pick up speed.

"Oh, it was great, very cool. I nearly missed it though."

How come?

"Well, you know what it's like," explains Jared. "I had a few beers with a friend last night and so I overslept this morning. What a mad rush to get to the terminal on time! I made it with barely minutes to spare."

Well, I'm glad you made it, I reply, trying not to sound too concerned as a father. After all, I remind myself, Jared has hitchhiked on his own through Africa.

Travelling from Taiwan to the U.K. via the U.S. to visit friends and then catching a ferry ride to Canada is nothing for him. He has loads of experience on how to change plans and adapt to circumstances while on the road.

Just barely into our three-hour journey, I pull over for a fix of Nova Scotia's famous coffee. When we flew over here the first time, I say to Jared in a muffled voice, trying to chew on a doughnut and drink my coffee at the same time, we were so impressed.

We were blown away with the bays, islands and endless lakes. Then when we met the people, we knew we were in a special place. I want to introduce you to some of our friends. They're great.

"Cool," replies Jared, staring out the window while his left hand, almost with a mind of its own, grabs the last doughnut from the box between us.

As we negotiate the back roads and weave around the endless bays, each vista is awash with a palette of autumn colours. The season of splendour marks the end of the heady days of summer and beckons us to partake in the cycle of dying and renewal.

We spend a few days at our home on St. Margaret's Bay.

I notice that Deborah and Jared engage easily in deep conversations about travel, cooking and just about everything in between.

Although things seem easy between me and Jared, I decide to hold off on any discussion about exploring our relationship with each other and how my views about religion have changed until we take off on our five-day road trip around Nova Scotia and Cape Breton.

I hope our conversations will be easy but sense they could be challenging. I remind myself that the mantra of our business is to encourage leaders to practice "authentic dialogue" in the workplace.

I realize it's another thing entirely taking it to heart and practicing it with my own son.

~Chapter 4~
Taboos

Breakfast has come and gone. I enjoy a dark roast at the Blomidon Inn, the historic B&B in Wolfville, Nova Scotia, where we've spent the first night of our road trip. I follow a simple routine I've done thousands of times before: I taste the coffee, I lean back, stare into space and ease into a comfortable holding pattern as the caffeine slowly disperses the fog in my brain.

Jared is sitting opposite me at the breakfast table, archiving and deleting pictures on his digital camera. A stab of urgency interrupts my reverie. During his year teaching English in Taiwan, Jared put aside money so that he could get to Canada to see me before going on to the U.K. to teach.

I sense he has expectations that we find each other anew on this road trip. I too have expectations that I will begin to understand where he is coming from as a gay person. I'm not sure how this will happen. How should I initiate our important conversations? And we have just a few days before Jared leaves for the U.K.

After loading our bags in the van, we drive west, taking the back roads through rural Nova Scotia towards Annapolis Royal.

It's the first week of October. A smell of wood fires is in the air. A grey-blue sky surrounds us as we glide along in our hired van, its burgundy exterior blending with the colours of the season.

Autumn leaves, dressed in yellows and reds, swirl and pirouette on each side of the road as we pass.

The fields, stitched together like patchwork quilts, are getting ready for their winter respite, knowing that Mother Nature will soon wrap them all in layers of downy snow.

This is Acadian country. The expulsion and deportation of the Acadians by the British took place here some two hundred and fifty years ago, when the French-speaking settlers were shipped away from their beloved Grand-Pré and surrounding areas.

Now the fields and dykes are a place of pilgrimage and rediscovery for the Acadian diaspora.

I recognize that I too am on a pilgrimage — a road trip that leads within, not to find a god or a religion but to discover more about myself and to find my son.

I sense that what we are doing is profound in some way. With Jared's permission, I place a digital recorder on the dashboard between us to record our conversations. I want to preserve our time together.

We don't speak for a while. Trees, farmhouses and fields swish by. When the silences get too long, I become self-conscious. The longer the silences, the more difficult it is for me to break through the void.

I brought CDs along, lots of them. So did Jared.

I put on Van Morrison. I turn up the volume so the words of the chorus, "When it's not always raining, there'll be days like this," resonate through the van and ring in our ears. The mood lightens.

We engage in some small talk. Jared, aware that sooner or later we are going to get onto the subject of homosexuality, takes the initiative. He gets on a roll about God having a dialogue with self-righteous people about gays.

I am a little surprised he's using religion as a starting point as it can easily divide us, especially if we don't know yet what each of us believes. And if we get entrenched in opposing points of view, it could end our discussion and maybe jeopardize our road trip.

Jared puts on a God-like voice to tell a joke making the rounds in the gay community:

"You want to have another commandment?" God asks the people.
"Yes," the people reply in unison. "We want Thou shalt not have sexual relations with a gay person."
"I don't think we should include that as a command," God replies.
And the people cry out, "Please God, make that one of your Ten Commandments. We really feel strongly about that one on Earth. We wish that you had reflected that better in your Ten Commandments, rather than Thou shalt not kill."
"Please, please God," they cry out, "remove Thou shalt not kill and replace it with Thou shalt not have sexual relations with a gay person. We really feel strongly about that one."
All is quiet. God thinks. Then comes the reply.

"I am quite set on Thou shalt not kill," says God.

"No," cry the people, "we don't feel strongly about Thou shalt not kill at all. We really want to kill."

Our raucous laughter fills the van.

Hey Jared, I say, you've got me thinking. Instead of saying Thou shalt not, how would people react if some of the commandments were turned around to reflect our rights and responsibilities in a positive way, rather than focusing only on what we should not do?

Many of the commandments in the Old Testament are about social responsibility, but they are coercive. And negative coercion kills one's spirit. The "all have sinned" indictment is saying you are bad, bad by your very nature! How motivating is that? There's no acknowledgement of people in terms of their potential.

Surely it's better to turn the commandments around so that they gird one's potential, rather than assuming people are a lost cause right from the get-go. Instead of drawing attention to what one can't do, the emphasis should be appreciative, focusing on the solution, not the problem.

You know what I mean?

"Cool," says Jared, not wanting to get drawn at this stage into a heavy religious discussion. After some thought, he continues sarcastically, "But won't religious people feel short-changed if their religion starts to focus on the positive?"

Some might feel their thunder is gone, I reply. But others would welcome it. Hey Jared, imagine if the Ten Commandments were re-written reflecting universal values and human rights!
Imagine if the commands encouraged positive behaviours and outcomes!

The faithful would have a more realistic assessment of their potential and self-worth instead of feeling condemned when they miss the divine standard.

"When I was in Taiwan," says Jared, "I received an e-mail that was doing the rounds. It was a copy of a letter someone had sent to a religious talk-show host from the U.S. She had been ranting away that in the Bible, the book of Leviticus says that homosexuality is an abomination."

Oh, I've heard her, I say. What a bastion of self-righteousness!

"Some of the situations in the letter were quite funny. I sort of remember this one:

My neighbour is having an affair. In Leviticus it says that he should be taken to the town square and be stoned. We have Times Square here in New York. Should I get the police to do this or should I take the matter into my own hands?

There are quite a few variations of this letter doing the rounds but you get my point?" says Jared, looking across at me.

Absolutely, I say, laughing. It's amazing how gullible people are to believe a talk-show host who cherry-picks texts from the Bible to support her position, I say.

"Exactly!" says Jared.
He eases himself into a yoga-type position on the passenger seat and gazes at the quaint homes along the shore of the Minas Basin. He's animated. "What about all the other rules of the day during the time of Leviticus. Are we meant to follow those as well?"

I'm continually amazed, I reply, how religious talk-show hosts, especially on U.S. television, are so quick to tell others to do what they feel is the "right thing."

It's a convenient smokescreen that allows them to never look at their own lives. We should start with exploring how we make assumptions and govern our lives according to the rules in our own heads. I should know, having been a minister in a previous life—in case you'd forgotten?

"I hadn't forgotten."

Jared doesn't offer any more. I notice he doesn't show much interest in my previous life. His disinterest reminds me of how fundamental I was in my early years as a minister.

Like the talk-show host we spoke about, I was convinced I was on the winning side, God's side. I "knew" the Bible had answers for everything.

A sense of dread and embarrassment floods over me because I sincerely believed I had a mandate from God. And like a religious doctor, I naively prescribed scriptural solutions based on my world view at the time. I'm eager to tell Jared I have done some serious thinking about my previous approach to religion.

For one thing, I've learnt that there are no clear cut solutions that can be plucked from the bible and offered as a remedy or a condemnation. It's no longer black or white. There is a lot of gray.

As the sun starts to burn away the clouds, I realize that those years of living in a fundamental religious fog are behind me. I can choose to wallow in wasted years or learn from the past and move on to new things. It's my choice. And at some stage on this trip I need to let Jared know what I believe now and how I've changed.

With one hand on the wheel, I pull my sunglasses out of their case. I look at the rural scenery, searching, but not seeing. There are no cicadas to provide a backdrop of sound, as you get in Africa. Instead we have the hum of the tires on the road, and a Jack Johnson refrain that draws us into a mid-morning contemplation.

After a few songs I say, speaking of Bible punchers, I read recently that a road sign in a town in Texas reads "Support New Testament Morality." I had no idea Christian religious conservatives in the South wield such enormous influence over the way people think. And especially the way they control the content of school textbooks.

Apparently the Texas Board of Education members have enormous buying power, and they're able to influence publishers to change what they consider immoral references. For example, any hint of a reference to gays or gay relationships must be changed.

"Really?" says Jared, searching for the lever on his seat. He eases himself backward, to the point where he can only see the sky and the tops of trees whizzing by.

Oh yes, I reply. So publishers change the word "partners" to "husbands and wives," and "attraction to others" becomes "attraction to the opposite sex." These conservatives take it upon themselves to practise a form of censorship so that kids will not be exposed to "unseemly" ideas and relationships.

Meanwhile, they have such lax attitudes towards gun control that kids can get handguns and assault rifles to blast teachers and fellow students when their egos take a beating or they get pissed off. Just blows me away. S'cuse the pun.

After a pause, Jared looks at me as if to say, "Where's this leading to?" Relieved that Jared hasn't dozed off, I continue. Other conservative groups try to reposition the natural history of the world to fit their view that the Earth is only six thousand years old. So in some Texas school books, the ice age did not happen millions of years ago but "in the distant past." Isn't that absurd?

"Bloody hypocrites," says Jared slowly.

And what is even weirder, I add, is the fact that because they have such enormous buying power, the edited school books are then sold to the other states because it would be too costly to alter them according to the whims of each state. So textbooks for many U.S. states are censored by a few powerful religious conservatives from Texas.

"It's so fucked up," says Jared, as he places his hands behind his head. Another long silence encircles us as we glide along.

I notice there's hardly any traffic on the road — only the odd farm truck and a delivery vehicle or two to the communities of Berwick and Aylesford.

Waiting for words, my mind meanwhile goes into overdrive. What about unchallenged rules spinning around in my own head — my prejudice against gays and the super religious? I really need to turn to the subject of homosexuality with Jared.

The longer I talk about other issues, the harder it becomes for me to raise the subject. I decide it's now or never.

Jared, I say, a little hesitantly, can we return to the idea of the absent father we spoke about the other evening?

Jared remains motionless, lying back in the front seat, staring straight ahead.

We spoke about your need for emotional connection and my being out of the home for long periods.

I know I wasn't there when you might have needed me during critical times. What sort of influence could that have on you being gay?

"You touched on that subject yesterday and I told you about my lack of confidence," replies Jared firmly. "I don't think I can make a link to your not being there as the reason for me being gay. That's not enough of a reason. It's got more to do with the way I interact with people and my lack of confidence. The things I do and the way I've learnt to interact with people are in a female way."

"It's got nothing to do with being gay, but if I am only around women and interacting with women — and they talk in a very different way, about very different things — it affects me. It's got more to do with role models."

I try to keep my eyes on the road as Jared's words sink in. When I glance over, I can see that Jared is sitting on his hands, leaning forward. I need to understand what he is really saying. His brothers had me and his mother as role models as well, but Jared was the neediest of all.

And I didn't notice. As a minister, I was juggling so many balls at the time. I was often away from home and emotionally preoccupied with all the needy people around me. Is he saying that his mom was a stronger influence in his life and therefore she became his role model? Maybe that's what Jared is saying and he's just being nice because he doesn't want me to feel bad.

So do I need to beat myself up with guilt because I wasn't there for you? I ask hesitatingly.

Jared continues without really answering my question.

"I can understand your need to find a reason for me being gay, and what caused me to be different from what you expected. For me, it's no longer important. I can't find the root, and I have thought about it quite a bit."

Okay. Can you pinpoint a time in your life when you first knew you were gay? I ask.

"No, because I don't know what makes me gay," replies Jared. "And I think we partly like to think there was some change, like everyone is naturally heterosexual and something comes along in your life and turns you around. But I don't know if that is the way it really works."

A long, pensive silence fills the van. I know Jared is probably pondering my fascination about what caused him to be gay. Was I in denial when Jared was growing up? Did I ignore who he was becoming? Surely the signs were there?

Finally he breaks the silence. "Do you know what I am saying? It's the perception that each kid is born a perfect being, a little straight baby. What a nice little straight kid!"

Jared's voice goes up a pitch. "Then this kid grows up. And then one day the kid discovers he's homosexual. Another blemish on the human race! How sad."

I decide to change tack because I don't want to upset Jared. He seemed okay talking about his orientation until I asked him what caused him to become gay. Is he bitter towards me because he feels I'm part of the reason he's gay?

I decide to ask Jared if he remembers when he first became interested in aspects of the male body.

Jared, I say, think back to when you were about ten years old. Remember there was always a lot of joking around and laughter amongst us.
In particular, you had an impish way of referring to butts in your conversations that always got a laugh from the boys.

I remember trying to use reverse psychology on you, because it must have worried me that you often managed to swing the conversation and draw attention to a guy's butt, albeit in a funny way.

I remember saying, "Jared, if you keep on talking about butts I am going to get a picture of one and stick it on your wall." I guess I was trying to embarrass you.

"I don't think you said it once, you said it a lot of times."

I can't remember the context of those conversations, I reply, but I do remember that it did concern me at the time because none of the boys had the same fascination. But then again, maybe they had other boyish fascinations and maybe I didn't notice them because they either hid them from me or they didn't trigger the same response.

Do you remember that, Jared?

"Yeah, of course I do," says Jared, leaning out his window and taking a picture of himself in the side-view mirror.

I think to myself, I'd better go careful here. The last thing I need now is for Jared to interpret my questions as being in judgment of him, especially after he gave me feedback on my communication style last week when we were having dinner at the Rope Loft in Chester.

Jared said that when we lived in South Africa, I often took him out for breakfast, yet most times I was physically present but not really engaged.

And furthermore, when I am engaged, he says I tend to evaluate and make judgments before I have really listened to what he is saying and where he is coming from. That really pisses him off.

I would get pissed off too if I felt I was being judged way before I'd had a chance to be understood.

If I follow my old ways, our discussion will end right now and maybe also for the rest of our road trip. I don't want to risk that, because who knows when we will get together again? I can choose to drop the topic or pursue it. I'm still curious and tread carefully.

So, what was the fascination? I ask.

"You know," Jared replies, "all kids do that.

When I was in Taiwan teaching those little kids, there was no end to joking about shi shi, because those kids knew exactly what was taboo and what was not.

Whether it's shi shi for them or shit for you, we all have our taboos. But what might be taboo for you is not necessarily taboo for me."

I think to myself, He's right. It's a reflection of the rules in my head. What's taboo for me is not necessarily taboo for him.

We arrive at the B&B in Annapolis Royal in the late afternoon and spend the rest of the day taking photographs around Fort Anne and the streetscapes of Annapolis Royal.

~Chapter 5~
Doing the mileage

N ext morning after a slow breakfast, we take a last drive around Annapolis Royal before heading back eastward on the highway towards Cape Breton.

It's misty and grey outside, the type of day that gets me addicted to melancholy, as I sink into a vortex of self-reflection. And that's a conversation stopper for sure.

After about an hour, the light begins to improve. Better light means better photographs and better conversation. I notice a ten kilometre sign for Paradise coming up.

I turn to Jared. We might even find a coffee shop in Paradise, I say, trying to make a joke.

Jared ignores me, deep in thought. After some further reflection, he says, "I don't think if we explore our relationship, we are going to find a reason for me being gay. That is my thing to work out in life. It's not something that I am always happy to talk about, to have to explain and explain. I don't think we will find the root cause in our family."

The trees on each side of the road flash by. Endlessly.

"You understand what I am saying?

Things like work and identity, and family and heritage," Jared pauses momentarily, "these are things that are influenced by family, but I don't know how much my homosexuality is influenced by our family."

Well, it's only in talking that maybe something will come up as a possible reason, I say, forever hopeful that I will gain insight into Jared's same-sex orientation.

During this road trip, I continue, I want to find out more about the gay experience and try to understand it. Maybe I've been in denial, thinking you might grow out of it, maybe you'll change.

I went into an introspective stage and started blaming myself, saying to myself, "I was responsible for your homosexuality. I was the absent father."

I had all those thoughts swirling around in my brain, and at that stage we had not yet had a chance to talk. And the more I talk about it, the easier it is for me to accept it and not adopt a judgmental attitude.

Jared is staring transfixed at the road ahead. He doesn't notice the verdant fields softly glowing, as early-morning vapours filter out the harshness of the sun.

You know, Jared, it's not the easiest thing for me to talk about either, I say, keeping my eyes on the road.

"Carry on," says Jared, looking more comfortable with the focus on me and not wanting to interrupt the flow of my revelations.

When you told me you had come out, I was hoping it wasn't true and if it was, I was hoping you were going through a phase and that it would pass.

And in the beginning when our friends here inquired about you, it was easier at the time to make small talk without disclosing my sense of loss that you are gay. I figured it was my fault and a just reward for not being around when you needed me most.

I know I'm approaching homosexuality from a straight point of view, but my thinking has changed this last year. I'm at the stage where I can check my assumptions, you know. Now I ask myself, "Where do those thoughts about gay people come from?"

"How d'you mean, changed?" asks Jared, still staring ahead, then glancing my way as he undoes his seatbelt and reaches backwards to retrieve the map lying on the back seat.

I wait for Jared to buckle in and unfold the map. Well, for example, I say, from time to time I have gay guys attending my seminars. When I say gay, I mean sometimes they are overtly gay, in the way they walk and their tone of voice. Do you know what I mean?

"I get the picture," replies Jared, looking intensely at the map.

Well, when I have one of these guys in my seminar, my first impulse now is to interact with them in the same authentic way I interact with the whole class.

What I'm saying is, before I might have gone through the motions, and pretended I was genuinely interested and welcoming while I secretly kept a distance.

But now my response is sincere and warm because I'm thinking, that could be you sitting there. I'm no longer conditioned by the rules in my head.

Jared turns and looks my way, then back at the map. "Is this where we're headed, Margaree Forks?" he asks.

That's it, I say. It's off the main road. Yesterday was a winding back roads day. Today is more of a highway day, except we'll take the winding route around the Minas Basin to get to Truro. And then at Truro we'll get back on the highway to Cape Breton.

I wait for him to finish examining our route. I really want him to hear what I am about to say.

Before leaving South Africa, I say, I started to reassess my religious upbringing and my theological training. That process changed a lot of my thinking about what I accept and what I reject, and about sexuality. All these things have changed, Jared. I'm in a different space now.

"How come?" asks Jared.

I think to myself, How can I condense what was a big part of my life into a few words? I take a few moments to collect my thoughts.

For seventeen years, Jared, my mind was influenced by a theological degree and years of Bible studies, seminars and sermons. I eventually realized that what I believed was only relevant within the confines of a church or religious paradigm. I had no language outside of that. Do you get what I mean? I look across at Jared, feeling vulnerable.

"I never knew any of that," says Jared, staring straight ahead before turning to me.
No, I guess you couldn't have.

"We had one conversation on the phone when I told you, and then a year later you came home to visit. We had lunch and hedged around the subject a bit. And that was it!"

You forget, I reply, trying not to come across as too defensive, we did share stacks of e-mails.

"Yes, that's true."

The sun starts to burn through the early-morning mist. Signs of autumn are everywhere. Hillsides are alive with hues of orange and red. Neatly stacked woodpiles can be seen under covers in preparation for the long winter. The invasion of light brightens the mood in the van.

Where are you planning to stay when you get to the U.K.? I ask Jared.

"Brighton."

What's special about Brighton? I ask.

"Well, the most important," says Jared, "Brighton is where I've been offered the opportunity to qualify as a teacher. And secondly, a few of my friends live there already."

Are those mainly gay or straight friends? I ask.

"They're all straight. I've got stacks of straight friends and relatively few gay friends. Hopefully I'll meet someone there because Brighton has quite a large gay community."

That's interesting, I say, the fact that many of your friends are straight. Do you find you need to spend time in areas of a city that are gay to find gay friends? I ask.

"I remember in my second year at university. I was really frustrated because I had been through all the ups and downs of coming out to myself and all I wanted to do was jump in there and have some interaction and experience. But I didn't know anybody else who was gay at the time.

"So at that stage I remember having a definite need to find gay friends and to hang out with gay people. Growing up I wasn't exposed to anything very gay at all, and nobody I knew from school was gay either.

So one afternoon I drove past Café Manhattan, it's one of the more popular gay cafés in Cape Town.

I was heading back up the street when I thought to myself, 'Jared, you're always thinking about doing something about this situation.

It's now or never.' So with my heart pumping I made that split-second decision and did a U-turn and went to ask for a job.

That was a big turning point for me, because I got to meet a lot of different gay people.

So in that sense, I needed to gravitate to the gay area in Cape Town because I needed that little push to realize my gay identity publicly.

That's when I wrote 'Finding Gay Space' for my degree, you remember?"

That was a very good piece of writing!

"It was a bit different in Taiwan, as you can imagine. I went to Taiwan after being with Ali, my boyfriend, for a year. We had the best time and I still adore him very much, but when I left South Africa I was hungry for something new and exciting.

I hadn't been very confident at all in Cape Town, and I was looking forward to meeting lots of new people and enjoying the natural confidence that comes from being a stranger in a foreign country. So in that sense, I specifically chose Taipei over a smaller town or village, because I wanted to check out the gay scene in the city. I wanted to visit some of the gay clubs and bars.

But at the same time, it's all a little superficial. I do enjoy going to some of the gay bars and restaurants in a city, but the atmosphere is very specific, it's all about getting sex.

So sometimes the whole scene can be a bit much. I end up getting too drunk and doing stupid things. At the same time I'm beginning to want another Ali — someone I can have as a friend as well. I've never really been any good at the whole one-night-stand thing.

That's very much part of the culture there, and with the added politics of white and Asian relationships."

How easy is it for you to be yourself and single when you're with the crowd? I ask.

Jared continues, either not hearing my question or ignoring it. "So at the moment I'm quite happy to be by myself. Of course, I enjoy meeting new gay people when I have the chance, and that happens more regularly now that I have built up some confidence in myself.

Relationships for me are easier when I see someone socially first, outside of a bar. It's like building a bridge. That way it's much easier than trying to get your personality across to someone in a crowded and noisy bar."

I realize Jared has answered my question in his own way. I'm glad he feels comfortable enough to talk about it.

Hey Jared, I say, trying to catch his eye. I just want you to know I appreciate what you're telling me.

Jared glances at me and pulls a face.

We weave through a swathe of large maple leaves that have spilled over the embankment and onto the road. I glance through the rear-view mirror. The leaves, now swirling, settle back in new patterns. I notice that slowly but surely, in fits and starts, our conversation is developing its own subtle rhythm.

Have relationships got easier since you've come out? I ask.

"I vividly remember my twenty-second birthday bash back in Cape Town. Birthdays seem to distil all my feelings about where I am in life, and I went into overload that year because I wasn't sure who I was and how to create my own space as a gay guy. I went out for drinks and saw the guy that had fucked me up from here to Sunday for a whole month."

I glance at Jared and notice that he's getting animated.

"I got really depressed and went home. I felt really, really down. I crawled out of bed the next day. It was way too melodramatic and all for nothing.

"But things have changed. In terms of creating my own space, I'm getting better and better at just being me and doing what I want to do. Now I enjoy hanging out with my straight friends and have great evenings dancing in the straight clubs."

Still seeing no sign of a decent coffee shop, I pull over under a magnificent maple, so that I can focus on what Jared is saying. The leaves, flaunting their fiery shades, dance on the glass. We watch the silent play for a few minutes.

Jared continues. "Living in Taiwan has been a great confidence booster for me. Creating my own gay space is something that I'm trying to do all the time. To be gay and to be me at the same time, without having to hang onto the gay scene as a crutch, if you know what I mean? Being myself as a gay person is one of the biggest challenges of growing up. I think I'm getting better at it all the time," confesses Jared, looking my way to see if I'm paying attention.

I risk a question. Do you need to tell people around you that you're a gay guy?

"Establishing my gay identity is an issue no matter whether I have a partner or not. It's not that I feel like I need to establish it. I don't make a concerted effort to tell people. Straight people don't do that either. I enjoy having a little secret when I meet new people.

But I know it will inevitably surface in conversation. So at this stage, I'm cautious to tell people. If it comes up in conversation, then that's cool. I have no qualms about it.

It's just one of those things that people get to find out when they get to know me. And I find that more and more, I need to be public about it. It's something that is changing with every relationship I have.

I'm finding it harder and harder to separate myself from my gay self, and it's getting easier to be honest about who I really am in front of people without being ashamed about that fact.

But, of course, it's still difficult in certain situations. And mostly it's my own issues. The odd thing is that when people find out I'm gay, they instantly warm to me. I'm their new best friend. Yet at the same time, I don't enjoy being put into a box. And even though everyone else in a group is totally fine with my being gay, in some ways I still feel like a sore thumb.

But that is part of being gay in a society that is conditioned primarily to support straight people.

Being gay is not going to go away, and I'm getting better at recognizing that feeling and moving through it. It's not going to change, and the more I am public about being gay, the easier it gets, although here and there, I still have a sense of shame. But I try not to withhold who I am when I'm with straight people either.

Mostly I find that I am only as restricted as I restrict myself. Straight men, especially younger guys in the cities, are so used to having the gay element around that they don't care that much anymore. It's just a matter of pushing my own limitations when I get into a situation in which I feel particularly different.

People accept people who accept themselves!" says Jared, looking at me with self-assurance.

We'd better get moving, I say. I start the van and drive slowly onto the deserted road. I'd still like to know more about your understanding of a gay identity, I say.

Are you saying you're now grounded enough in your gay identity not to need someone else, like a crutch, for affirmation?

"I think I'm grounded enough in my identity not to need someone. I am at a place where I have more fun by myself and enjoy spending time on my own. The kind of relationships I'm looking for are ones that are easygoing and easy to fall into.
They feel natural and right, and I can mix these easily with my sense of self. Part of being gay is being single and enjoying relationships when they come your way.

There is a definite single syndrome in gay culture and partly because some gay relationships don't last that long. There are of course wonderful exceptions. I don't see myself as needing somebody else to confirm my own identity.

I prefer to think of wanting someone to supplement me. Who doesn't want a fulfilling relationship? Whereas before, I was dying for some kind of interaction, but never having the confidence to pursue the people I liked.

Now I'm finding myself quite happy to have some kind of choice in the matter. The only thing that contradicts this is a feeling of loneliness. That's normal I think in a foreign country, and in that sense, who wouldn't want someone to spend some time with? I don't think you could call that a crutch though. It's just human."

It's lunchtime. We stop for coffee and a bite to eat at a mom-and-pop restaurant overlooking the waters of the Minas basin.

Although the décor is plain and rustic, the atmosphere is welcoming. It's like popping in to see Aunt Jane.

Once the waitress has brought our order, I turn to Jared. You've really helped me understand what you've been going through in trying to establish your identity as a gay person.

I lean across the table and whisper: Were there times while you were in Taiwan, Jared, when you felt tempted to try the other side? I mean, you were sharing the apartment with two other girls. Did you ever feel the faintest urge to sleep with them?

"I've never had sex with a woman."

So, when one of the girls brought a guy home, didn't you feel a bit jealous? I ask, ever hopeful for a small sign that Jared could be bisexual as well.

"No," responds Jared flatly. "Of course not. We'd all be rooting for her to score!"

We laugh.

Coffee arrives. The locals drift in and out, the screen door slamming each time.

I try to imagine living in an apartment with two girls and guys coming in and out. It's a different world out there, I remark.

You're obviously in a space where what goes on is accepted, I say, trying not to sound judgmental in any way.

"I guess so," says Jared, turning to me. "I guess I'm looking at a big generation gap right now."

Okay, okay, I say. I try to ramp up my image a bit and explain where I'm coming from.
When I was your age, Jeez, I sound so old when I say that, I made out in the back seat of my car. It was the same girl. There was none of the revolving-door sex you're talking about.

"Too bad," says Jared with a smile.

After paying the bill, we wander back to the vehicle. Most of the mist is gone. We lean against the van, heated by the sun, warming our backs.

About what I just said about revolving-door sex, I say after several minutes. Jared turns to me, opening one eye.

I realize it's not only gay people, in case you thought I was labelling all gays as promiscuous, but heterosexuals are doing exactly the same.

"Everyone knows that," says Jared, "but just like you thought, many straight people think it's only gays who sleep around. And that's not true."

Hey, I guess I knew that but point taken. So here's a question, and this has nothing to do with one's sexual orientation.

Weren't the girls and you afraid of picking up AIDS? I ask.

"No," replies Jared firmly, "because everyone wears condoms."

That's a relief, I say, getting into the van.

Jared opens the route map and says, "So what's the plan?"

It's best we get onto route 104 once we get to Truro, I reply, otherwise we'll never get to Margaree Forks before it gets dark.

Jared gets out his Kings of Convenience CD and places it in the player. We settle into a mellow groove.

After a few minutes I say, I don't want to come across like I'm prying into your private life, but I'm trying to understand how you lived in Taiwan.

Don't you feel a bit odd if there's a strange guy, someone the girls dragged home the night before, in your apartment the next morning?

"We definitely want to see him leave the next morning, because then we can bring out the dirt on him. It wasn't only about that, of course . . ." says Jared with a laugh.

Up to now, I say, I've never had an insight into that aspect of your life. I do remember feeling pretty out of touch and helpless when you first arrived in Taiwan, because there was nothing I could do.

I knew you were in this strange city, strange language, you were low on cash, you'd rented the wrong apartment in a seedy area, then found another one and were trying to find someone to take over the first one.

And I'm thinking, "He's got to get money soon 'cause he has to pay rent."

"Then why didn't you phone and say, 'Are you okay?' Something like, 'I was just thinking about you, in a strange city, what's it really like?' would have gone down well," retorts Jared, a little upset.

I did try on a few occasions, I reply. Remember, you didn't have a cellphone yet and when I did call, you were often out and a stranger would answer.

Once you got your new apartment, we did have contact at least once a week, I add, trying to place things in perspective.

Jared ponders this as we drift along. Silence, except for a tension in the air and the hum of the tires on asphalt below.

"And then, I come to Canada and meet your friends and the feeling I sometimes have is that you like to cherry-pick the good things about your sons. You know, 'These are my son's achievements.' And sometimes I feel you haven't done the mileage with me, but you want to cash in on my achievements. You highlight my achievements and downplay the fact I'm gay."

What do you mean, I haven't done the mileage with you? I ask.

"What I mean is that you weren't around when I was struggling through stuff and when I got my degree. You might have helped with money, but you weren't there in person. You have to earn the right to speak about me and be proud of my achievements and the fact I'm gay."

Hey Jared, isn't that a bit harsh?

Jared doesn't answer and grabs another CD. I decide to back off in case I come across as being too defensive about not being around when he needed me.

We spend the next few hours talking about the music we've brought along and listening to each other's CDs.

Just as Jared is about to have a big yawn, I see the sign for the B&B at Margaree Forks flash by. I shout, There it is, and pull over to the side of the road.

Jared, still trying to complete his yawn, says, "At last."

Before we check in, I say, you were talking about me doing the mileage with you, and then I interrupted you . . .

"Oh yes," says Jared, "I nearly forgot. I thought it was just enough for me to tell you and Mom. But it's not, you know. Mom said to me, and I didn't think it was important at the time, but now I think it is. She said to me, 'If you come out, I have to come out too.

It's not enough that you come out, I've got to come out too as a parent of a gay son.

And that means that every time I meet a new person or interact with people at work, my friends, it's not that I have to make a big deal of it, but I can't hide it.'"

Jared turns to face me, leaning against his door. "So you've got to come out as a parent of a gay son in your day-to-day conversations.

Like the time one of your woman friends came up to me and said, 'How old are you? Wow, Jill is also 23, maybe you guys can get together sometime.' She didn't know!"

Jared, hang on now, I say.

"I don't expect you to tell everyone, 'Hey, I've got a gay son.' But she didn't even have a clue."

I sense Jared's disappointment. I push my seat back to stretch my legs. Let me explain, I say. I don't remember who I have told and who I haven't told.

I'll give you an example. At the end of a party one night in the middle of winter last year, three of my close friends and I were wallowing in a hot tub out on the deck in the snow. The wives had all gone inside already and were making coffee.

And we're sitting there drinking wine and talking about all kinds of stuff. That's when I told them I was looking forward to your visit and that you were gay. These guys were so accepting.

When I told them, I presumed they would tell their partners. But they didn't because maybe it wasn't a big deal for them or they were respectful of keeping confidences. I don't know.

"Which is absolutely right! They should keep confidences" responds Jared.

So, I continue, I presumed the word would get around in this small community and obviously it didn't. Look, every one of my friends that I had spoken to about your visit knew you were gay.

"I'm glad," says Jared, less indignant.

One or two people might have slipped through the cracks, I say. The integrity of these people, their sense of community, has been a healing thing for me. So I've not been embarrassed at all about telling people you were gay. I even told people at work!

"And what was their reaction?" asks Jared.

They were all very accepting and open about it. You know, if I wanted to hide it, I might have told people that were close to me, but not people who had an influence over my career! I hope you understand that I'm not embarrassed about the fact that you are here and you're gay.

"That's very important to me."

A Complicated Love

~Chapter 6~
Blank space

I t is past 7:00 p.m. on day three of our road trip. We've had a good day taking photographs and exploring some scenic areas on the Cabot Trail.

Although we haven't covered many kilometres in comparison to yesterday, I feel Jared and I have closed some gaps between us, just by hanging out together.

We check in at a local B&B in Baddeck. After dumping our bags, we head for a restaurant on the main road. We find a quieter spot against the far wall of the restaurant. The music is loud enough for us to talk without anyone listening in.

Let's get back, I say, choosing my words carefully, to when you spoke about the need to feel grounded, the need for an emotional connection. Does your concept of feeling grounded include a need for a sense of place as well?

"Feeling grounded about myself, having a sense of self is part of it, but it's also the need for an emotional connection to a place or a home," says Jared pensively.

What you're saying touches a nerve with me, I confess. The only way I can describe it is that it's a sense of loss.

"What do you mean?" asks Jared.

I'm trying to get to the bottom of this, I reply. It's a sense of loss for the memories that we could have created together.

"That's it," says Jared. "Good memories are a backdrop for me. I tap into them whenever I want. Do you know what I mean?"

I know exactly what you mean, I say. When I look back on my childhood, sweet memories is the one thing I wish I had more of as a kid.

To myself, I think back to my first marriage and all the years that I felt like an alien in my own home. My marriage was in a mess. As an escape, I spirited myself into a twilight world, away from the daily grind of trying to maintain a relationship that had run dry on love.

Jared interrupts my reflections. "A sense of making history together. That's what I was looking for. We never really got it together," reflects Jared.

That's part of the loss, I say. And in addition I have to deal with the fact that we left our homeland for good reason and you guys are not around us anymore. Do you remember you mentioned not having a sense of place in one of your e-mails Jared? Well, after I divorced your mom, I started to feel more energized when I met Deborah.

That's when things started to change course. We decided to buy a house, hoping you guys would feel more at home there.

But you never really did. You came more out of a sense of duty, only because it was my weekend.

"Maybe the reason why we never felt it was our home was because we were never part of it," states Jared, with conviction, looking at me.
I guess so, yeah, I reply.

"We were never there," says Jared, leaning forward and tapping on the table with his spoon.

Yeah, you were never there, I repeat.

"If we had been there, if that was our home, maybe you would have thought, 'Hey, this is a home because my kids want to be here. Why would I want to give this up? My kids really like it here,' " says Jared, waving his hands toward me like a priest conducting an absolution.

Okay, I get the message. It was a big sin, I say. But how would you have felt part of it? Should I have involved you more in the purchase? That's why we settled for a house closer to town, but not too close, I remind Jared.

"I don't know," replies Jared, flipping trancelike through the menu. Now in retrospect, it's easy to say, "Oh, we should have done this or that."

You probably weren't aware that I was going through a bit of an upheaval at the time.

"We had our own stuff to worry about, getting through the year, passing our exams," says Jared.

At that stage, I say to Jared, I was wondering, what do we do? Stay in Africa, and face the future with a good chance of minimal personal security, having to watch our backs each time we want to smell the roses?

If we stayed, we had a house that was rising in value, in a good area. But it was a barricaded house. It had high walls, an alarm, an electric gate. Maybe it would never become a home. When you feel you're under siege, there's no guarantee your house will become a home.

The alternative was "the dream," to find a place in Canada and buy a home near a lake or on an island. We knew it was a gamble. We were hoping we could carry on where we left off. But we underestimated the emotional disconnect when we didn't see you guys on a regular basis. And that's why we need to talk like this and spend time together, I emphasize.

"You once told me you moved around a lot as a kid. So, if you didn't feel grounded and connected to a place, why didn't you stay and build on what we had instead of emigrating to Canada?" Jared asks rather angrily.

Good question, I reply. Now, looking back, I realize how important it is for me and you to build a relationship.

But then it was below my radar.

It was very hard for me to create something that I didn't know I had been looking for myself.

When we decided to come to Canada, I say, it was a difficult decision. We realized we would be giving up our financial security for a sense of personal security and peace of mind. The price we paid was that we had to "abandon" you guys for a while and start all over again.

That's the sense of loss and the painful part for me. I provided you with the basics, such as rent, university fees, but I couldn't provide the most important part, the emotional support and connection.

"But why not emigrate a few years later, when we were all a bit older?" asks Jared.

I remember discussing this with you guys back then, I answer. In ourselves, we were torn, because we were sensing that South Africa was not our home anymore. We were feeling more like aliens in our own country. And that's mainly because of the rampant crime.

It was a Catch-22 situation. The longer we waited it out, we would lose our eligibility because our age would count against us. Another reason was the predictions at the time that the South African rand would continue to devalue against the U.S. dollar.

Of course, 9/11 changed all that, but it was a fact we had to consider at the time. The longer we put off emigrating, if the currency kept devaluating, the fewer savings we would have left to build a new future for us and you guys.

I say "you guys" because the fact we are Canadian citizens now could be a big comfort and benefit to you in the future.
We were thinking about you, you know.

The waitress brings two glasses of water, a tradition in Canada. She takes our order. We both choose the same meal— oak-planked salmon, rice, veggies, home-baked bread and a pint of the local draft.

I'm already eyeing the crème brûlée for later. I continue on the subject of "home."

Jared, you once mentioned female figures in our family who kept the traditions going and the family together.

"They are the only ones who stuck around long enough," replies Jared with disdain. "I don't know where you were."

My mother, your grandma was there when you came home from school, right? I ask.

"For us, she was the person who was always there!" says Jared emphatically. "I went to play piano at her house. I would go there after lunch and hang out with her and her dog and go play ball.

When she moved into the suite at the back of our house, she is the only person I can picture. I see her everywhere in that place. I remember her everywhere."

She was an amazing person. She had the gift of making anyone feel special, I add.

"And somehow I don't remember you there, at our house. That's about it," says Jared, with a sense of regret in his voice.

Silence. Jared's words sink to the bottom of my soul as his shadow dances lazily on the wall to the flicker of the candle.

You don't remember me? I ask.

"I'm sorry, but I don't," replies Jared.

The reality of what you're saying is pretty hard to hear. I'll have to think about this for a while, I conclude.

"I suppose so," says Jared.

I feel a deep sadness welling up from within me. Nothing I say will change the reality that Jared has no memories of me in that house. The waitress brings our beers.

I look at Jared. Your mom and I were not in a good space at the time, Jared. I remember now how I felt more comfortable away from the shouting and the tension. As a result, I became physically and emotionally detached from the place. And unfortunately, I saw you guys less and less. It was no longer a home to me.

"Well, the fact is, I don't have many memories of you from that period."

I think to myself, I don't have many clear memories of my parents being there for me as a young child either. But they were there.
The memories just aren't that clear. If you do have memories of Grandma, I add, and not of me, she was obviously filling an important need.

"I've got lots of memories, things me and the boys used to get up to. I don't have many memories of you in our previous house either. The only memory I have of you is when Mom threw the ketchup bottle at you and it went through the window."

Gee, I don't remember that. I must have deleted it from my memory, I reply.

"She threw the bottle at your head and it broke the window," says Jared, laughing and fingering the tomato sauce bottle on the table as he recalls the moment. "That scene is etched on my mind."

I really don't remember that, I confess to Jared. So many things were thrown at me. It's a blur.

"Well, it's the only thing that stands out in my mind!" says Jared.

Shit, the only memory, I say. Well, it could have been worse. You could have no memories at all, Jared. At least you have one of me!

I realize my attempt at humour doesn't work. I'm actually being defensive.

I think of all the photographs I have of Jared and the boys.
Maybe if I show these to Jared, he might recall some of the good times
we had together.

After some reflection, Jared says, "Maybe memories of you are there
deep down, but it's not something I draw on. If they're there, I don't
know where they are. It's not important to rehash all that. What I'm
really trying to say is, there's a blank when it comes to you."

Gee, thanks, I reply sarcastically, savouring the reality that I, an absent
father, am a "blank" in Jared's past. No memories, no good times, just a
blank. I feel a deep sadness and sense of failure permeate my body, its
emptiness gnawing at me.

 Thanks to a book I read recently on how to have clear conversations, I
consciously resist the urge to defend myself, or retreat into a cocoon and
beat myself up about it. Instead, I decide to park my emotions, and try
and hear what Jared is really telling me.

Our meal arrives. I order more beer. We don't talk as we tuck in. I weigh
in my mind whether I should remind Jared about all the things we did
do together, the places we went to, the hikes we took. After giving it
some thought, I decide not to.

I don't want to come across as trying to justify myself. And anyway, it
won't bring back the memories.

Returning to the question that has haunted me since I learnt Jared was
gay, I eventually break the silence.

If I wasn't there for you during those formative years, I ask, how much impact did that have on you, not having a male figure to bond with? What impact did that have on your sense of identity? It must have had an impact.

"How am I supposed to answer that question when I don't know what I didn't have?" Jared responds angrily. "You want me to measure the impact? We've already gone over this.

I don't think that we're ever going to find one simple influence or lack of influence or a single reason that people are gay. People are gay for a variety of reasons. Each person is gay in a different way. There are different influences that make us gay. And there's a continuum of sexuality, from hetero to bisexual to gay and lesbian and everything in between. Genetics is a factor and self-esteem issues and the dynamics of one's family."

We both immerse ourselves in thought again. After about ten minutes Jared breaks the silence. "I think the dynamics within the family are the least important."

You do? I ask. I think to myself, Maybe I'm just too eager to be absolved from playing a role in Jared's homosexuality. I can't stop blaming myself for not sensing and responding to Jared's struggle for identity.

Why do you say that? I ask

"Well, for all sorts of reasons. But I don't want to discredit the whole idea of a lax father, resulting in a lack of influence, you know."

It's quiet in the restaurant. The servers are so busy, they don't notice the music has stopped. A lax or absent father? I ask, self-conscious that someone might overhear.

Jared doesn't reply.

I sense Jared's disappointment in me and his internal conflict. He wants to tell me that I wasn't there for him as a role model when he really needed me the most, when he was struggling to find an identity. Yet I know he doesn't want to hurt me. Have I sent a message to Jared that gays are inferior and that he's not special in my life? If Jared is disappointed in me, is it reversible? Can I restore my relationship with him?

To change the subject slightly, I say, You hinted in a previous conversation that bonding with guys is a search, in a sense, to connect?

"Are you asking or telling?"

I guess I'm probably asking and telling at the same time, I reply.

"If you're asking, then yes, of course, I have a need to connect," responds Jared.

In one of my e-mails to you I mentioned that some of us search for a match in a partner. Do you remember what I said about the imago?

"Sort of, but you'd better refresh my memory."

I want to revisit it briefly to see if there's a link with my being perceived as an absent father and your need to connect.

"Go for it."

Okay, bear with me. The imago match is all about a composite image that each of us has of our parents and early influencers. So, picture this.

You're sitting with this wonderful new guy at the bar. Now remember, I mentioned our subconscious brains have an embedded image of the good and bad aspects of our parents and those early influencers.

Let's say you feel attracted to this person because you discover you have similar ideas and interests. You get the feeling of deep comfort, you feel romantic, energized, it's like you have known this person forever.

As you talk, your subconscious is matching up similar aspects of your parents, in this case, your mom and me, with this new beau, because it wants to complete the unfinished conversations you never had.

And because the subconscious doesn't act as a censor, all the faults and virtues of your parents and influencers are projected onto this new and potential lover.

If the match is non-threatening and positive, if it feels good, comfortable, familiar, and if it resonates with you, the chances are you'll want to pursue the relationship.

Why? Because the root of your attraction for this guy is driven by a strong desire to bring the relationship to completeness, to continue the unfinished conversations you never had with me or your mom and other influencers in your life. Maybe that's why they say, "Love is blind."

"So, what's your point?" asks Jared, unconvinced.

Maybe your strong desire for a relationship with a guy, I say with enthusiasm, is driven partly by a need to complete the relationship with your parents, especially me.

The waitress brings fresh-brewed coffee and takes our plates to the kitchen.

Jared adds milk and sugar and slowly stirs his coffee, staring straight ahead. After a while he replies, "Um, I don't think so."

It's not a conscious thing, I add. It's an emotional need to bond, to connect. The need to find one's imago match applies both to straight and gay people.

"No," says Jared assertively, "because the things I would talk about with you are not what I would talk about with a boyfriend or with people I am attracted to. We don't have the same type of conversations."

Okay, I say, but it's not the content or type of conversation I'm talking about, but rather a subconscious need for emotional connection.

In this case, it's with your boyfriend, because you didn't have it with me. In other words, because you didn't have that need met with me, you project it onto your boyfriend, with the expectation that he meets this need.

Jared takes a sip of his coffee and looks away. "I don't know," he says, sounding sceptical.

It's not a rational thing that you would say to your partner, I reply. "Hey, I have these unfinished conversations."

"If it's not rational, how am I supposed to know about it?" asks Jared indignantly.

It's just a theory, I reply. You know about it usually after the event, when you start analyzing your motives and reflect on why you were attracted to a person. I never had a sense of connection with my father, and when you are in the middle of it . . .

"I am in the middle of it."

Okay, I reply, when you are in the middle of it, it doesn't make sense.

We both remain silent for a while. The waitress brings the crème brûlée.

Jared sighs and makes an effort to move the conversation forward.

"You're always asking, 'What about male influence in your life?' It's not so much about male influence.

It's more about a father's duty to be there, to be available!" says Jared.

Yeah, I know, I say resignedly. But I can't do anything about that now.

"If I look at the role of parents, the mother's role is to dry your eyes and make sure you're fed and take care of a host of things. But the father's role is to teach me about having an identity as a man. Who I am! What is my heritage? What is my role? These are our traditions!

My ancestors are these people and this is where I fit in. That gives a sense of belonging!

So, if I think about my relationship with people, with my partners, at the beginning it was mostly for a sense of self-worth. I'm attracted to the people I would like to be. And it's been those people that have strong families and strong cultures, exotic people. I search for partners who are totally different because maybe their family and their reality is better."

That makes sense, I say. I'm conscious the music has ended and we will be overheard. I lower my voice. You sleep with someone because you want something from them, right?

"Yes and no," replies Jared. "Sometimes it's mutual. You both want to give and receive. Not because I think that person represents aspects of my father and therefore I want to experience the relationship I didn't have. With me, at times I have a low sense of self-worth, so I think, 'Maybe I can get that from someone else.' "

You having a low sense of self-worth—is it because we were pretty disconnected during those vital years? I ask, not really wanting to hear more about my shortcomings, but unable to let go of this idea entirely.

"A part of self-worth is having a place in the world."

And you didn't feel like you had a place? Do you think that was because I might not have made you feel special, like you belonged?

"Maybe," replies Jared.
You were always an astute observer, on the sidelines, I add. You observed our family saga and its breakup. You watched as your security was swept away in front of your eyes.

And what made it worse, I think, is that your mom confided in you. You were like a young sponge, absorbing the trauma. I'm concerned that you now see me through her eyes, from her perspective, if you know what I mean.

"That may be so," replies Jared, "but I have no way of knowing."

This must have had a psychological impact on you, I say, because you weren't mature enough at the time to take sides or to take a step back for perspective.

A series of sepia-like images flash through my mind in slow motion. As I see his mother and me having endless heated disagreements, I imagine Jared absorbing the negative energy like body blows to his heart.

It makes me want to rewind the tape and start again. Despite my inner resistance, the overwhelming sadness that's been growing throughout the evening threatens to envelop me.

"It did," replies Jared softly. "You have no idea what that fuck-up of a marriage breakup did to me."

Each of you reacted differently to that mess, I say, after a long pause.

You were always reading and were aware of things way beyond your years. You have an incredible capacity for connection, and I realize I missed the opportunity to connect with you when you really needed me.

"Yes, you did."

A Complicated Love

~Chapter 7~
The ultimate screw

Today is the fourth day of our road trip. We eat a slow, wholesome breakfast at the B&B. Everything seems to be happening in slow motion. Our lethargic state is due in part to the late night — I played guitar and Jared read — and a half litre of wine we enjoyed in our suite after supper.

I am pleased with the depth of our conversations so far, although I feel emotionally drained when I reflect on how little Jared remembers of me in his formative years. How many opportunities for genuine connection did I miss because I was preoccupied with my stuff?

And that calls into question my role as a father to all my boys. Like a misspelt word in a Google search, would I come up as an error reading or a "blank" if they were to google their minds for instances of when I featured in their lives? "I'm sorry, your search returned no results. For a better result try 'Real Father.' Still no result? I'm sorry, it appears there are no recorded instances of 'Real Father' in the database."

We pack the van, wave goodbye with promises to return someday, and head for the Fortress of Louisbourg, the National Historic Site on the eastern seaboard of Cape Breton Island.

Mindful that today is the second last day of our road trip, I have no set agenda for today except to understand Jared better and to connect with him in a more meaningful way.

And if the last few days are anything to go by, I will end up learning much about myself as a result of our conversations.

After an hour of Cesaria Evora and Diana Krall, I switch to Yamandu Costa. A surge of Brazilian guitar rhythms and delicious licks fill the van. The fog lifts.

More energized, I turn to Jared. Hey Jared, I know we've talked about some of this before, but I'd like you to fill in some of the gaps for me. You once mentioned in an e-mail that your previous boyfriend was an extension of you. He was everything you wanted to be. Were you saying that because you lacked self-esteem at the time? I ask.

"Let's put it this way," replies Jared. "I don't think that's a defining characteristic of my sexuality. I noticed that was happening."

Has that changed? I ask.

"I think so."

So, how has it changed? I inquire.

"Well, I didn't want to be a clone of my boyfriend," Jared replies after some thought.

Okay, given what you've just said, do you still have an "urge to merge"? In other words, a guy might seem so attractive to you that you're prepared to sacrifice your own sense of self, your own needs, in order to get his attention?

"No, of course not!" exclaims Jared.

How have things changed then? I ask.

"Things have changed because I never had a real relationship with anyone before," says Jared. "I only had fantasies about people. And the odd sexual experience. But it wasn't a relationship. They were just encounters. So it changed because I didn't have a fantasy about my relationship with him. When I spoke about people I was attracted to, it was more about the fantasies I had about them. The kind of people I thought they were."

That's very interesting, I observe.

"The difference is when I met my previous boyfriend in South Africa, it wasn't me fantasizing about someone else," says Jared, "it was us coming together and having a relationship."

Makes sense, I say.

"When I left for Taiwan," continues Jared, "we sort of broke up but it never really got into my brain that we would never get together again. I knew that we wouldn't, but somehow I believed we would at some point.

Then when he met this other guy, I realized I must move on and he must as well.

I feel guilty because I could have gone back. I was the one who left in the first place.

And I wonder why it's only when I'm not with him that I want to be with him. You know—absence makes the heart grow fonder.

When I was there, I was so busy making plans to get away that I took him for granted. We had good times but I didn't give him what he deserved—my full attention."

Sounds like me: when I was with you, I didn't give you my full attention, I observe.

"Right. All I can say is that it's too late now. I'm sorry, but it's over. You had your chance. I had my chance," says Jared with finality.
I guess so, I say.

"And I have to stop relying on my ex-boyfriend for support. It's not fair and I have to try to move on. But it's hard because ours was the only real relationship I've had."

Both of us remain silent. I think about how open Jared has been and how difficult it must have been for him to talk about my failed relationship with him and his relationship with his boyfriend.

I don't remember ever having open conversations like this with my father. I wonder how many of my friends can say they had frank discussions like this with their parents, caregivers or children.

"And by the way," Jared continues, "is it uncomfortable for you to talk about my boyfriend? No biggie. I was just thinking about it yesterday."

My mind flashes back to when I first knew Jared was gay. I wrestled then with the possibility of Jared and his boyfriend coming to visit and staying over in our guest room. Images of Jared lying in bed with his boyfriend come to mind.

I turn towards Jared. In the beginning, I reply, it was hard for me to visualize you having a boyfriend, let alone saying the word "boyfriend."

But it's getting easier as I go along.

"Good," says Jared, staring straight ahead. I notice he looks relieved. A smattering of rain lands on the windshield. The grey clouds seem to jostle each other for position in preparation for the changing of the season.

Every few minutes the sun breaks through, charging the autumn landscape with blazes of colour. Each to his own, we muse along for another hour or so, until we spot a welcome sign above another mom-and-pop restaurant up ahead.

It's time for an early lunch. We find a table at the window overlooking a stretch of rocky coastline and a tempestuous sea.

I find I want to know more about Jared's sex life and how it compares to my experience of heterosexual sex. To my chagrin, I realize I never had discussions with Jared when he was a teenager about relationships, love and sex.

Hey Jared, I say, you're probably going to think I've a fetish about sex, but I want to ask you a few questions about gay sex and how it compares to my experience of heterosexual sex. Here's a ground rule though: if you feel I'm asking uncomfortable questions, tell me to back off or mind my own business. Is that okay?

"Shoot," says Jared. "It'll be interesting to see what's lurking in that devious mind of yours."

I laugh. Point taken, I say. So, picture this. Here's a guy, he's gay, and he's having sex with his gay partner. If he's young, he reaches a climax and after a while, depending on his age and virility, maybe more than an hour, maybe less, he has sex again. I'm saying this, hoping that I haven't lost touch with my understanding of male virility.

"Right, it's part of being a guy, a virile guy," says Jared.

When I was younger, I confess, I could have sex five or six times a night. But I never realized, until much later, how inexperienced I was. The quality was bad, very bad. But, talking about virility, as I get older, multiple orgasms don't happen anymore, at least not for me. The buildup period takes longer. Now I've learned to make the journey much more interesting.

"Like shoot, aim, fire," jokes Jared.

No, nothing like that, I reply.

I stare out the window, my mind momentarily flooded by memories of my early days of primordial, driven sex.

But a woman, I say, her experience is totally different from a guy. A guy's ability to have multiple orgasms fades with time, but if she's in a relationship where she feels comfortable, loved and safe, she may have multiple orgasms in one lovemaking session.

That's one lovemaking session! And here's the upside for women. She can continue having orgasms like this till she's in her sixties or older. That's where a skilled lover can be worth a lot more than his bank balance.

I look at Jared to see if he's paying attention.

If a guy knows, I continue, that he is capable of only one orgasm for the next few hours, he will spend time making sure that she has a series of orgasms, as a buildup to sharing one massive orgasm together. What keeps him excited during lovemaking is her journey of buildup and climaxes to mutual complete fulfillment. It's the full service treatment, Jared.

So, here's the question, if that can happen between a man and a woman, what happens between two gay guys? How does it work?

"Each gay experience is different," replies Jared. "I'm still young so I definitely can come more often than once a night."

I'm so glad to hear that, I say in jest.

"Like you said, younger men can have multiple orgasms," says Jared, "but with gay guys, their experience is different. You can have an orgasm while you're getting fucked, but even if you don't have an orgasm, it still feels good. And if the person that is fucking you has an orgasm, then a little later you can have sex again and swap around. It depends on the couple."

I notice our waitress hovering. I guess she wants to take our order. We both scan the menu, and place our orders. I realize that she had brought the menus and glasses of water at least ten minutes ago. That's why she was keeping a respectful distance. She must have overhead our dialogue and not wanted to intrude.

A woman, I continue, has very sensitive areas around her vagina, her clitoris and inside her vagina, particularly her G-spot. The whole area is a minefield of sensitive nerve endings!

"Never been there," says Jared, without even a hint of sadness.

When you're getting fucked, I ask, does pressure on your prostate give you a pleasurable experience?

"Um, sort of, but there are a lot of nerve endings around the anus as well," replies Jared.

But are they nerve endings linked to sexual pleasure? Does the brain interpret those sensations as sexual? I ask.

"Definitely," says Jared emphatically. "Some guys get an erection when they are being fucked. Other guys don't. So if you come with your dick, that's one way of coming, but if you come with a dick in your ass, that's a different type of coming altogether. You come in your ass."

How do you come in your ass? I ask, bewildered.

"The centre of sensation is felt more strongly in your ass."
I look across at the swells rolling in. I try to visualize what I've just heard. But, if you're getting fucked, can you still come with your dick when the locus of sensation has changed? I ask, still trying to grasp an image of two guys fucking.

"Right! You feel it in your ass."

So the locus has moved? I inquire.

"It's a different kind of orgasm," replies Jared. "And it's very powerful as well."

When a woman is being fucked, I explain, she can have a vaginal orgasm, she can have a clitoral orgasm or both together.

"I don't know anything about a woman's organs," Jared confesses. "But it's definitely pleasurable to get fucked by a guy. Some guys can continue getting fucked after they have come, others can't. The important thing is there are many ways to be sexual. Not all men have anal sex."

I never knew that. It's very interesting, I reply, dazed by what I've just heard.

"Yeah, your ass is really sensitive. If you're horny, then the sensitivity in your ass increases."

What about kissing a guy? Does that bug you? I ask, trying to imagine myself kissing a guy. It bugs me.
"No, not at all!" Jared replies.

It wouldn't be a turn-on for me, I confess, no matter how hard I try. Just the thought of a guy all over me would make me want to get away as soon a possible. But having said that, I'm not against being close to a guy, you know, like a biblical Jonathan-and-David type of relationship. As long as it's not sexual.

A long pause. We both stare at the few condiments on the table.

What about guys with beards? I ask. Do you like a beard?

"It really depends on the guy," Jared explains. "I'm not attracted to men with beards. I was kissed once by a guy who had a beard, and that was a real turnoff. But a guy with a bit of stubble is a turn-on."

I think about male-to-male attraction and all the gay people I know. Some are friends and associates. I try to visualize kissing any one of them. I can see myself hugging, no problem. But kissing? No way!

"I've got friends who are attracted to hairy men with beards, so it's different for everyone. Guys with beards are not something I'm into."

What do you think about older men who keep young and vulnerable guys going with money, accommodation, food and gifts in exchange for sex? Isn't that taking advantage? I ask, trying to move away from the subject of guys kissing each other.

"It's more complicated than that and it depends on what country or area you're talking about. In Thailand, for example, there is a definite positive economic impact because rich foreign fags come for a week of sex with a local Thai guy.

It happens with straight folk as well. People go to exotic places just for sex or an old guy provides his mistress with all her physical needs and money in exchange for sex."

I guess you're right, I say.

"That's not the kind of relationship I'm attracted to though. I don't know what it's like to be an older gay man running out of options. I'm not in a position to judge. The thing about being gay is being young, being youthful and having a nice body. If you're not in a secure relationship when you start to fade like that, having a young fuck-boy around is a substitute for loneliness," explains Jared.

Lunch arrives. Our waitress asks if we want coffee now or later. I reply "Now and later, please," conscious that we might be here for a while yet.

I realize there's still a lot I don't know about gay relationships. I say, If you fancy a guy you meet in a club, how long does it take before you are having sex?

"That would depend on the guy and my state of mind. If I really liked him maybe I'd wait a while. But if I was really horny or a bit drunk we could end up going home that night."

I know I'm harping on this, but what about AIDS? Do you take the risk or is it only protected sex? Or is it only blow jobs and hand jobs?

"I've always used a condom, except with my boyfriends after we've both been tested and waited the window period."

Gee, that's good to know. That's something I worry about with all you guys, I say, feeling relieved.

"It's no big deal. Condoms 'r' us," says Jared jokingly.

We laugh.

I continue. I find that parts of a woman's body turn me on big time. Maybe it's because I don't have a woman's body, but there's a sense of mystery there. How does that work for you if you are with a guy? Is there still a sense of mystery?

"I'm not sure. I think I have a pretty good understanding of how a guy's body looks and works. There is a sense of mystery in that he is a totally different person to you, with different feelings and desires."

Remember our ground rule Jared. If I'm asking too many stupid questions, tell me to back off or buzz off. Okay? You've been amazingly open.

After a brief silence, I continue, What turns you on about a guy's body?

"Well, it would depend on the guy, but I can get turned on by almost any part of a guy's body. Obviously there are some areas that I like more than others."

Do you think you could ever become bisexual, you know, "any hole will do"?

"No, I don't think so at this stage. It's not really about fucking a hole for me but about being with another person. Maybe your question has more to do with your need to have some kind of hope or understanding than with my desires. I'm just not attracted to women, though many men would have sex with both."

Our waitress, waiting for a lull in our conversation, moves in swiftly to fill our cups.

Okay, Jared, I say, stretching my legs sideways across the chair beside me. Help me understand what goes through your mind on a one-night stand, when you want to pick someone up.

"It's not something I've done a hell of a lot," Jared replies. "I wasn't going out and having sex every weekend! I've only slept with a few guys and fooled around with a few more."

Okay, so, how does "it" happen? I ask.

"You mean?"

From a heterosexual point of view, I explain, let's say I'm at a pub, I strike up a conversation with a woman, I get on the dance floor and things usually go from there.

"It's pretty much the same."

Would you be at a gay club or a straight club? I ask.

"It would be a gay club."

Okay, have you ever picked up a guy at a straight club? I ask.

"No, but I don't see why not," replies Jared. "Oh! But I have, when I was in Thailand. I picked up a guy at a straight club. It's not that I have a sex plan that I go with. Things just happen. I probably should have a plan that works. When I was out drinking and clubbing one night with my friend, we ended up at a club where I met a guy on the dance floor . . .

And I met another guy on the Internet, in Taiwan."

If you meet on the Internet, do you arrange to meet somewhere?

"Of course!"

Okay, so you're having a date with a guy you met on the Internet.

Do you give the full treatment on the first date?

I'm conscious that Jared could at any moment tell me to fuck off and mind my own business.

Jared, unfazed by my question, replies, "It depends, you know . . . It depends on the person. Sometimes people don't want to go that far. And as I said before, if I like the person, I don't want to sleep with them straight away."

Right, like you said. I take a breath. I am about to broach a rather private and potentially "messy" subject. It's now or never.

Okay, I say, so here's my problem. When you both agree to have sex, it's not the most hygienic act ever invented. I once read a gay sex advice column and the subject was anal sex. Someone wrote in and wanted to know when you are having anal sex and you catch a whiff of doo-doo, do you carry on like nothing has happened?

He was asking if this was normal and what does a gay guy do when it happens? Is it game over?

In reply, he coined a word, I think in "honour" of some American dude. He said it was not crap, but "santorum," that was messing up the ambience.

He then told his reader that this was perfectly normal and gave instructions on what to do when "santorum" happens. I thought to myself, I helped raise you guys and I've changed a good few diapers.

Even the faintest smell of santorum while making love would put me off totally. Okay, Jared, so how do you deal with santorum in a gay relationship?

Jared looks around the restaurant before replying. Our waitress is keeping a safe distance.

"No, it doesn't, it's never been a problem. The anal sex I've had, I've never seen or smelt santorum. Now, if you know you are about to have sex with a guy, and if you feel constipated, you don't have penetrative sex, pretty much the same as with a woman, with her periods. And when you do have penetrative sex, it's not smelly, there's no santorum, and you're using lubricant so there's no smell."

Isn't there always a risk of that? I ask, realizing that I'm coming across as totally anal. That's it, I'm fucked, a shrink will have me for breakfast.

"Maybe, but I haven't experienced that. But I admit it's one of the first things you stress or think about when you're about to have anal sex," Jared confesses.

I think to myself, I would never, ever be able to get round to having sex with a guy, let alone having anal sex.

I know there are straight guys, I say, who have anal sex with girls. They must have the same fears, I guess.

"That's one of the first things people think about. But I don't think it's really an issue. You smell lube, and that's it."

Anyway, I confess, here endeth my inquiry into the world of gays and anal sex. I'm not talking about it anymore. I'll get over it, I joke.

"Your narrow little perspective on the world of gays," says Jared with a smirk, "has come to an end. Now you are enlightened. Go out into all the world . . ." he says, imitating a TV preacher.

We both laugh and pause for a moment, gathering our thoughts while the waitress pours more coffee. Once she departs, I say, Jared, I really need to say how I appreciate you being so open with me.

Jared looks my way for a moment and then begins to slowly stir his coffee. Then, almost in slow motion, he puts the spoon down and looks at me and says, "Okay."

Relieved, I continue. You know, Jared, when I see a woman's naked body, in good shape, it does something for me. Although I can appreciate a Michaelangelo-type body, there's nothing in me that wants to touch. How is that different for you?

"The desire that you have for a female body is the same desire I have for a male body. It's hard for you to imagine, but you need to turn it around and see that the desire is there, just another focus."

I remember an article I read about testosterone and the male brain, I say. It said that every person begins life with a proto-female brain and genitals. And some individuals end up with a low-masculinized brain, a male body but with a female brain. Jared considers my question for a moment, then replies, "I haven't known anything else."

I can understand that, I say. But if you've never had sex with a female, how can you be sure you're not missing the ultimate screw?

Some women take so much pride in their vaginas, I swear they take their vaginas to the gym! You've no idea what it's like, Jared! Surely an asshole can't come close, excuse the pun?

"I can ask you the same question," says Jared. "If you've never had sex with a male, how do you know what it's like? Maybe if you try it once, you might find the ultimate screw with a guy. It might blow your mind!"

I've got no desire and it's probably the same with you.

"Right! It's not that I haven't thought about it. I have. I'd only try having sex with a woman out of curiosity's sake. I wouldn't even know how to come on to a woman," Jared confesses.

Okay, let's say you are in a situation where a woman is coming on to you. She doesn't know you're gay. What then?

"I wouldn't say no. I'd have to see what I'd do in that type of situation when I get there. But I don't know how I'd ever get into that type of situation!"

You told me about a situation where this girl was lying on your bed waiting for you to take some action but you missed the cue because you didn't clue in to the signs she was giving.

"Yeah, so what?" responds Jared.

Well, as a single guy, I'd give myself a serious talking-to if I didn't recognize the signs and missed an opportunity like that.

"One of my gay friends said he got drunk with a woman and they had sex. He said it was fun, but it wasn't his preference.

It didn't turn him on. I'm sure that in the next couple of years, given the opportunity, it might happen to me. And that will be great. But don't get your hopes up."

I lean back in my chair. Interesting, I say. I can appreciate you saying there's no surge, no energy, no rush. I'm trying to understand it from your perspective. I suppose it's because I've never been in your space.

"That's the thing," explains Jared. "It's not that I'm attracted to all guys. I'm attracted to a certain type of guy, with a certain type of physique.

I'm sure it's the same with you, there are a lot of women you don't want to see naked. They don't turn your crank. With me, even if a woman guarantees me the ultimate screw, no matter how beautiful she is, naked or clothed, it's a non-starter, a non-event. Get over it."

With our meal concluded, we depart and after a short drive, arrive in Louisbourg in the early afternoon. After dumping our bags at our B&B, we spend the rest of the day exploring the Fortress of Louisbourg National Historic Site.

Four days and a few hundred kilometres can't hope to make up for so many lost years. But this journey is about new beginnings. We set out on the road almost as strangers, our dialogue awkward and guarded.

We've both revealed much of our authentic selves, our deepest hurts, despite the pain of revisiting our past.

If I were to rate our conversations in terms of what I've learnt on a scale of one to ten — about the gay experience, about Jared and about myself — I'd give our road trip so far an eight, because it has exceeded most of my expectations.

I've learnt a lot and also know I need to get over the fact that Jared is gay, he is my son, and he will eventually find his own space as a gay person in the world.

~Chapter 8~
Connecting

B arely five minutes into the final day of our road trip, we get the urge for coffee. I do a quick U-turn and pull into a coffee stop on the edge of Louisbourg. Jared comes back with two cups, freshly brewed, and two brown bags of doughnuts.

But we've just had breakfast, I complain.

"Good," says Jared, "then I'll eat them all."

Not so fast, pal, I retort, grabbing the bag.

"Okay," announces Jared, talking above the crackle of paper, "I think we should talk about how we've been communicating in the past. Let's talk about when you phone me. When you phone again, it will be so good if you really ask for details, like you mean it. And say something like, 'And how is Anna?' "

Who's that? I ask, conscious that Jared has taken the initiative to get communication going on our last day.

"She was one of my roommates when I was in Taiwan!" exclaims Jared.

"And remember her name! And then when you next call, and if you ask after Anna, I will be very impressed because you actually remembered her name!"

Realizing I've fallen into a trap by not remembering her name, I try to make light of the situation. Anna, Anna, oh Anna, I exclaim, beating her name into my chest.

"Anyway, the thing is this," says Jared, unimpressed by my little attempt at drama, "you think we're not interested in what's going on in your life. Well, the same goes for me. I don't tell you what's going on in my life because when I do tell you, you don't seem interested and you don't remember!

You don't remember my friends' names. That's so important to me! I saw a few guys in Taiwan. You don't know who those guys are, you don't know anything about them! You know nothing about what we were doing and who the person is I'm seeing right now."

I guess I don't, I reply meekly. I attempt a recovery. There was this one guy I knew about because you sent a photo of the two of you.

"Can you remember his name?"

No, I can't remember. Wasn't it Chan Lee or Lee Chan, or something like that? I ask.

Jared ignores my last comment.

"I'm saying this is important to me! You never phoned and asked, 'Who's that guy and what's going on between you?' "

Maybe I was avoiding making an issue of it. Maybe I didn't want to find out, I reply.

"Okay, I understand," says Jared.

It's so obvious, I think to myself. Why should Jared want anything but normal parental love and engagement?

Jared stares straight ahead as we negotiate the curves along the road. He eventually breaks the silence. "What I'm saying is that it's important to me that you know there is someone in my life."

You're reminding me, I say softly, how important it is for me to be involved in your life.

"Go figure," exclaims Jared.

The image of Jared's lover comes to mind.

When you sent that photo I admit I was disappointed, I say, because as a father I had a preconceived idea of your ideal partner, even a guy, and this guy didn't come close.

"What do you mean, 'He didn't come close'? " Jared says indignantly. "You don't even know the guy!"

To be honest, I say, after I saw the photo, I pushed it out of my mind. I guess I was thinking "Because I'm disappointed, I don't want to ask, and I don't want to know."

"I guess so, yeah. You don't want to know," repeats Jared, his voice trailing off sadly.

Looking for words, I attempt a reply. When I saw the photo of this guy I thought, "You can do better than that. It's not a match."

"But your son's having a relationship! Forget whether it's a match or not according to you. You need to know about your son's relationship!" says Jared emphatically.

I know I need to know, I say, because I'm a parent. But I also didn't want to know. I couldn't put the two of you together, if you know what I mean.

"So you 'saved' it in a folder in your mind?" Jared asks cynically.

I guess so. And I didn't want to bring it up now because you might think, "It's all about my father and his needs. He's not really interested in me and my partners." I confess I'm behaving like a typically paranoid father.

Here's the issue, Jared. For example, when a daughter brings a guy home, the father often goes ballistic when he first sets eyes on this guy because his idea of a perfect match and his daughter's are totally different.

His mind goes into a panic. He's thinking about his little girl, his pride and joy whom he's nurtured all these years. His worst fear is about to happen.

He knows this guy is a predator, and he's about to corrupt a beautiful young girl — his daughter.

So he gets into an argument. "Just who is this guy? Does he have a job? What does he do? Why does he have a metal ring hanging from his nose?

That's a breeding ground for germs if I ever saw one! If you wanna catch the plague, go ahead, kiss him. You wanna know why? I shouldn't tell you this, but for your own safety I will. All the bacteria you need for herpes and other diseases ooze from his nose ring and sleaze down to his lip!

I hope you don't ever, ever think of kissing that guy!" And on and on. All fathers think like that. It's because they know that this guy has only one thing on his mind.

Jared, unmoved by my eloquent portrayal of a father's love for his child, turns towards me and says, "You know what my response to that is."

Okay, Jared, I continue, I don't know the guy, but it's my prejudiced, fearful response, I confess. I'm telling you up front that's what it was.

"You see how . . ."

I interrupt Jared. Here's the end of the story. The daughter, however, thinks this guy is the best thing since the cellphone was discovered. She goes off and fucks the guy anyway, sincerely believing this loser is the only one who really understands her.

Now, I know with guys, I continue, it's different because fathers are less protective and tend to freak out less over their sons' relationships. But it's similar for me in the sense that it triggered responses in me.

I didn't know how to deal with my reaction at the time and didn't inquire because I feared it would become an issue between us. So instead of getting into an argument with you and alienating you, I avoided the issue. I guess I numbed out.

"For me that's not good enough for a parent-child relationship," says Jared.

Well, with you it's no longer parent-child, I say.

"Yes and no, you know. I have lots of friends and I don't envy their parent-child relationships at all. Just because many have crappy relationships doesn't mean I have similar expectations!"

So some of your friends have bad relationships with their parents.

What's your point? I ask.

"Well, it comes back to the fact you don't ask me about what's going on in my private life. And I know there are millions of parents out there who don't want to know what's going on in their children's lives. But because there are many who don't want to know doesn't mean it's okay not to ask!"

So, based on what you've just told me, I'll try and change that, I say. I'm getting to accept that you are very comfortable being with other gay guys. It's a reality, right? And we are talking about it. After this week, I should be able to talk about it much easier.

"Well, I hope so," Jared adds pensively.

I am in a much better space now, Jared.

"I hope," says Jared, looking wistful. "It's not only about, oh yeah, 'Who did you fuck last night?' What about my friends? They're important to me but in your eyes they're not important!" says Jared heatedly.

I bet some of your own friends don't want to ask you who you fucked last night either! I quip.

"No, no, no," replies Jared, "we talk about it endlessly, the ups and downs and ins and outs of it! I'm saying, you need to ask about the people who I work with and the people who are my friends."

You need to understand, I say, you were in Taiwan. And I should have been a concerned parent and pumped you for more information! All I know is that you eventually shared an apartment with two girls who hailed from the U.K. and the U.S. and the three of you became good friends.

When I phoned you, you often told me you'd had a wild party the night before and that you were sobering up. It seemed to be a recurring pattern every Sunday.

But when you told me you were working like a dog at the time, that was the only thing I could relate to. The names of your friends and the places you were going to seemed so foreign to me. I admit I was far removed from your world.

But now that we're talking, I feel more comfortable about asking you more questions.

"Here's the thing," says Jared. "If you want to have a long-distance relationship, those are the things you need to ask about! You've got to get in there."

I'm hearing you, I reply. I was worried that you might think, "All he wants to know is, who is this guy I'm fucking? Has this guy got AIDS? Am I practising safe sex?" Boring!

"You need to realize that the conversations we've had over the last four years have been conversations according to Dad! And they are these subject matters," says Jared, imitating my voice.

"So, have you given any thought to your future, Jared? Are you planning on going back to university to get your master's? It's lofty dreamy stuff, so I shift to speaking on your level and after a while I shoot, 'We had a really good party last night . . .' But you don't seem to hear!"

We don't talk for the next ten minutes. Instead, we gaze at the mottled countryside, lost in our own thoughts. I think about what Jared has just said. Do I really not hear him? Do I control the conversation?

I eventually break the silence. If you remember, Jared, in the last few years before we emigrated, we did spend time together. But maybe that was too late to have any influence?

Jared does not reply.

Do you remember our Saturday dates for breakfast, once or twice a month? That's when I checked in with you about what was happening in your life. And we did some great hikes together! That's better than most fathers, I add, looking for confirmation.

"Yeah, maybe . . ." Jared says very quietly.

"You can't confuse going through the motions with really being there. I think it's different."

I'm not sure what you mean, I say, reminding myself to not get defensive.

"I'm saying that there is a difference. Going out for breakfasts was not a substitute for being there. We can go out for breakfast every Saturday and not get to know each other. You know what I mean?"

Yeah, I think so, I reply, my voice trailing off.

I think to myself, *When I muse over things, I tend to shut out everything and everyone around me. The breakfasts became a comforting ritual, a way of structuring time.*

But they have no emotional connection or meaning for Jared, because I wasn't really there, fully engaged and interested in what was important to him at the time.

I attempt a partial recovery.

I have, I say, about seventy of our e-mails saved on my hard drive. I can't believe that we wrote so many. There was one e-mail, Jared, where you said you have to milk me for information. Do you remember writing that?

"Yes, of course. This is how the conversation goes when you write."

Jared leans forward, then pauses for effect: " 'Life goes on, we've got two cats and I've been thinking about this and that . . .' And I write back, 'What have you been thinking about this and that?' And you e-mail back, 'I have been thinking about this and this and that.' And I e-mail, 'So, what have you been thinking?' You know what I mean?" says Jared, clearly frustrated.

Okay, I acknowledge, there's not much detail, no heart stuff. You have a point!

I think about what Jared has just said. *Why don't I disclose the type of information he really wants to hear?* I never saw my father cry, out of happiness or sadness.

I remember watching early Clint Eastwood movies.

When the hero was in a difficult situation, he rolled his cheroot to the other side of his mouth, and then without any sign of emotion, he blasted the hell out of the bad guys. That type of stoicism and lack of emotional expression from early caregivers and influencers must have rubbed off on me somehow.

Can it be that I inadvertently cordoned off my soul, like an isolated outpost, unaware that real emotions, like talented immigrants, are welcome in the new world?

"Maybe you think we don't care about what's going on," says Jared, reaching for a CD. "The fact is that I've had conversations with the boys and all of us have found that we've tried to have a conversation with you, but we get nothing back."

Well, that worries me, I reply.

"And we don't know where our information goes. It's a black hole," says Jared, making a sucking sound. "It never comes out the other side. The reply is never 'This is what is going on in my life.' " After a brief pause, Jared continues, "I don't think much of it anymore, because I've learnt I wasn't getting much back."

Jared leans back and folds his arms.

We both fall silent. "Hotel California" by the Eagles is playing. The chorus gets to me. I know I can check out of this conversation anytime, but it would be extremely bad for me to avoid hearing what Jared has to say about my style of communicating.

After about ten minutes of staring straight ahead, I turn to Jared.

So I didn't often disclose what was going on in some of those e-mails. But there were reasons for that. If I go into that now, you'll think I'm making excuses.

"It's gotta work both ways, right?" says Jared, getting excited.

I'm hearing you.

"It's gotta work both ways," Jared repeats. "It can't just be 'Update Dad, click, send.' 'Update Jared, click, send.'"

Yeah, I know I haven't shared long e-mails with you, I respond. It was easier to phone. When you were in Taiwan, I tried to get hold of you every Sunday. I tried, but I couldn't always get hold of you.
"I know, I wasn't always there."

So at that stage, I add, I was trying to disclose more. In your first and second years at university, you will remember, I wasn't able to get hold of you that often either.

"I know," responds Jared, "and that's when I was going through a lot of stuff, the intellectual challenge, the emotional turmoil and plus having all kinds of responsibilities."

But it also works both ways, I add, choosing my words carefully. The reason I didn't go into detail was twofold. First, I didn't want to burden you with some of the stuff we were going through.

We were trying to establish ourselves in a new country and it was quite a struggle financially, with no network to get our business up and running.

Secondly, I wasn't sure if we were going to make it. If you remember, we were supporting you guys back home with rent and varsity fees, and I guess I was probably in avoidance mode, so I deflected your questions and gave a few superficial answers.

"That's a weak excuse!"

I guess the real reason I was distant, Jared, is because I was in survival mode for the first two years. I have a habit of insulating myself from you and others. It's a coping mechanism, my way of protecting myself until I've worked through an issue and I'm ready to talk about it.

Usually it's financial pressures that hammer my self-esteem. So when you'd ask, "So how are things going?" I didn't want to burden you with— shit, Jared, "We had five contracts cancelled this month, we're competing in a new country against people who have thirty-year networks, our backs are against the wall, the car is broken again, our credit line is getting maxed out, and we have to find the cash before the end of the month to send you guys for your rent and varsity fees."

And then underlying all this, I'm wrestling with some real issues, Jared. I'm asking myself questions like, "Is this what I want to do with my life?

Where do I fit in this world? How can I contribute in a meaningful way? What's my unique gift? How do I find my passion?"

Do you get the picture?

I feel both relieved and embarrassed about what I've just told Jared. We both fall silent.

I think to myself, *Why do I feel embarrassed? Up to now, I've always kept my own struggles and vulnerability hidden from all my kids. Why? It may well be that my lack of self-disclosure is based on fear: if they see I don't have everything worked out and if they see me as I really am, they might distance themselves from me for not being more "together" as a father.*

After about ten minutes, Jared says, "Can you see how this disconnect happens when we don't have enough context? I had no idea you were going through that. Shit, man!"

Jared looks away, deep in thought.

"Here's another example," Jared continues. "You never mentioned you were rethinking your beliefs, right?"

No, I reply. I was re-evaluating my beliefs in South Africa, and since coming to Canada, I've continued with that. It's a process, Jared.

"Okay, so you're expecting me, Jared, out of the blue, with no information, to get a dose of inspiration and write, 'Hey Dad, just as an aside, how are things on the religious front?' It's not going to happen!"

Point taken, Jared. Two things: I didn't think you'd be interested in my religious beliefs, how they were changing, and secondly, I didn't want to make a meal of the inner struggle either, partly because it was not clear to me.

There are still areas that are not clear to me but overall I'm more comfortable with what I do and don't believe. To be honest, it required emotional energy for me to unwrap myself and articulate things, especially things I was working through. Obviously I was wrong not to share what I was going through.

"Yes, you were."

Is there hope for us connecting in other ways? I ask.

"Oh yes, a three-week canoe trip," says Jared sarcastically, "to make up for the last fifteen years. We can bond as we sit around the campfire each night, singing Kumbaya. I can hardly wait!"

I'm sorry about that, I really am, I say pensively. I know I could have done things differently. I missed some great opportunities, and I underestimated the potential impact I could have had in your life. Jared remains silent. I can see he is angry.

When you're in survival mode, I say, getting divorced, carrying so much baggage, you think of surviving and paying the next bill. I had no emotional space. My emotional tank had run dry. In the ideal world, I should have had emotional space for you guys. But I was running, running just to survive, every day.

"We can't change the past," says Jared. "The important thing for me is to talk about the sense of family. You say you want to create a sense of family and I'm saying it's a dream."

I collect my thoughts and after a few minutes I say, Jared, I know you're deeply disappointed right now that things between us did not work out as you expected. You have to cut me some slack. You need to give us a chance!

"I know," Jared replies, his voice softening.

Because it's not only about a sense of place, as we discussed before, although that comes into it. It's a relationship. We haven't had that, I say.

"Exactly. That's exactly it!"

I've read a lot about relationships, I say. Most of us go through a type of yin-yang relationship when we are young. We fluctuate. We connect mainly with one person, then we are drawn to the other partner or caregiver, and then back. Trouble is, we were not that close ever. You're right, Jared, we weren't.

"But here's the thing," replies Jared. "I have such a strong emotional bond with Mom. She was there when I had some stupid crush on someone. She knows about a lot of things. The two of us have been dealing with stuff forever. We have a relationship that has built up over a long time."

I wonder again to myself, because of Jared's closeness to his mother, how much of me he still sees through her eyes.

Jared continues, "How are you and I going to connect when I'm in the U.K. and you're in Canada? We won't know what's going on in each other's lives!"

We have to start, I reply. And we've spoken about this before. We can't go back in history and recreate a physical place. But what we can do is build on our relationship. I can't replace those memories you had with your mom, but I can add to them and bring a balance.

"It's not only about having a lack of male influence in my life," Jared explains. "It's growing up to become a personality. You don't know what space to fill. There's no model. There's no 'You're my son and this is where you fit in.' So I didn't have the space to grow into, if that makes sense."

Makes perfect sense, I reply. It's also a new area for me, because my father and I were never close. My centre also came from my mother and my aunt. I've never had a role model where it's okay to talk deeply with a guy, let alone one's father.

"History repeating," muses Jared.

Absolutely! And to break the cycle, I say, it's no good blaming the past. We both understand the background now.

Maybe we should stop analyzing and begin communicating and connecting.

I'm prepared to do it from my side, Jared, I really am.

"We'll see," says Jared, fixing his eyes on mine.

~Chapter 9~
Crossroads

After our road trip, Jared went on to the U.K. and entered the teaching profession. He became a schoolteacher and took up a post in Cambridge.

Deborah and I sold our properties and moved to Vancouver, partly because of the business potential for our consulting practice and partly because of the longer summers and outdoor lifestyle on the West Coast.

Although our road trip showcased our courageous conversations and the way we were arriving at a deeper understanding of each other, in many respects, our journey had just begun.

It is now three years later and our most recent conversations are no longer around the subject of being gay. A portion of a recent e-mail from Jared describes it best:

> I have wanted something from you for a long time. I feel that you abandoned me when I was very young, by not nurturing me as a child and providing a safe place for me to grow up, and by not making me the centre of your universe, but just one part.

> I think I deserved to be at the centre, for a while at least. Then when I was growing up, you were never around to show me the way.

We did things together, at times, but you were not there to give me the daily support and show me what this manhood thing was all about.

I've never felt that you loved me especially, or even that I was deserving of love.

And I'm afraid that over the years I've got into the habit of offering you things that I think will impress you, hoping that you will turn around and hug me and tell me I am the best thing ever.

And the irony is, now that I am an adult, you can no longer give me what I needed as a child.

We are two separate adults and that time is over. So, I need to learn to find my own way and find that love for myself.

When I first read Jared's e-mail, his words cut me deep. At first, I was in shock and then I became very sad. I thought we had covered so much ground together.

Then I realized that even though we had spoken about this in depth, since then, under the guidance of his therapist, he's given himself permission, maybe for the first time, to express his feelings.

The raw emotions and anger that continue to surface are true for him at this time.

While I continue to recognize and acknowledge my shortcomings, we both need to break new ground by replacing any limiting beliefs about our past and each other with new experiences together.
We are both ultimately responsible for our own destinies.

I take courage in the fact that each of my boys has responded to me as a father in different ways. And in the bigger picture, I see Jared's reaction as a positive.

So, will we continue to have honest conversations? Absolutely!

As we continue to explore our complicated love, our lives will continue to unfold, revealing us to ourselves and to one another.

A Complicated Love

~III~

Lessons from the road trip

A Complicated Love

~Chapter 10~
Coming out as a parent

I'm at a cocktail party prior to a two-day conference on emotional intelligence. I'm making small talk with one of the delegates when an old friend joins our group.

With drink in hand she says, "My daughter e-mailed me the other day and tells me she met up with Jared in London. She says he's teaching at a school in Cambridge."

She leans across and says with a twinkle in her eye, "I think she has her eye on him." She takes a sip of wine and after a slight pause, she says, "Does he have a steady girlfriend yet? Ever since I can remember, he's always had girlfriends. He's a popular guy, you know."

Now it's my turn to speak. Do I preserve the status quo and give some superficial news about Jared? "Oh, he's too busy to even think of getting serious just yet." Do I lead her further off track by saying "I think he wants to do his master's next year. That will keep him out of trouble for a good few years"?

Or do I explain, "Well, Marge, it's like this. Jared has never been interested in girls. He's gay"?

Our road trip helped Jared and me explore each other's stories. Our discussions, liberally dosed with laughter, anger and silence, helped us find a measure of understanding and common ground.

In the process we learnt about each other's perspective and the concerns underlying our respective points of view.

Our lives can be seen as an enactment of stories similar to a play. Some plays move quickly to the denouement. Other stories need more detail to elucidate the plot and to bring transformation and self-insight.

Using the metaphor of a play, Jared and I each brought our story and supporting arguments to our road trip — acts one and two. As the week progressed, I began to see beyond my assumptions.

It became more difficult for me to hold my position and stick to my script, because I was learning so much from our conversations.

I am reminded of what Jared's mother said to him when he came out. "If you come out, I have to come out too."

I can't deny a part of me. To deny Jared is to deny my own humanity. For me not to come out, I would have to push Jared away from me. And that is not an option.

But for me to come out authentically for Jared means I need to explore both of our stories to find sufficient common ground and a moral imperative for a new and emerging third story — act three.

In his book Learned Optimism, Martin Seligman talks about a method of inquiry that helps bring clarity to one's path by contrasting two outcomes.

The first, the painful approach, is a way of exploring negative and pessimistic assumptions and their ultimate outcome. The second seeks an alternative and preferred, optimistic outcome, for those who want to be part of a solution rather than part of the perceived problem.

So for me to be authentic, I figured I needed to follow a similar method of inquiry by contrasting two outcomes, both hypothetical, of course.

The first would be to not come out for Jared but to go through the motions to preserve a semblance of relationship with him. The second option would be to come out authentically for Jared. When I juxtaposed both stories, I could contrast the two futures and decide which aligned best with my values and my sense of human dignity.

Outcome one: If my approach to Jared's homosexuality was conservative and pessimistic, I would perceive Jared's gay orientation to be a real adversity and problem for me.

Why an adversity? In the recesses of my mind I sense Jared's gay orientation will reflect negatively on me because it reveals that I have failed him as a father. And if I have failed him, how does that reflect on my ability to teach others and maintain successful personal and professional relationships?

What are my real beliefs about gay orientation? Although my belief system at the time Jared came out was in flux and not clearly articulated, I at first clung to the social mores of my upbringing, later influenced by my years as a church minister.

In short, my conservative outlook on a gay lifestyle consisted of three points: it was immoral, it was against nature, and it was against the will of God.

Faced with my son's homosexuality, I had to seriously examine my beliefs and decide whether I wished to continue with the same approach I'd held without question for thirty-five years or open myself up to new research and fresh input.

If I held onto my conservative and traditional beliefs about homosexuality, it placed me in a dilemma, that of loving my son but ignoring or rejecting his way of life.

If I adopted this approach, it would lead to a Catch-22 type of relationship, with the possibility of an ever-increasing distance developing between us.

If I only associated with straight people, I would insulate myself from Jared's world and live my life in a straight world, albeit with blinkers on. I could also withdraw emotionally from Jared, cut him out of my world, and devote my time and energy to my other sons, who are straight.

Alternatively, as a family, we could be ever so nice but not real, pretending that Jared was straight like us.

This would help keep the family secret (Jared is gay). As a family we could have unspoken rules to never discuss his sexual orientation in public or in private amongst ourselves.

Then, when we were together as a family, at weddings, funerals, birthdays and holidays, Jared would be under pressure to act as straight as possible in the presence of guests and family to preserve our "honour."

Our selective inattention would ensure business continued as usual and we maintained our "honour."

Of course, behind the scenes, Jared would know he had to play the game called "honour." He would know the chips were stacked against him because he would have to fight a psychological burden that is almost too hard to bear — our collective disapproving gaze.

Our first payoff as a family would be to preserve our "honour" and win the game. Our second payoff would be to dehumanize Jared with acts of negation — to breed such low self-esteem and psychological pain that Jared would have no choice but to flee to his own kind to escape our stifling conspiracy.

This way, we would keep things "clean" by clearly drawing the line. Jared would stay out of sight and beneath the radar. And on rare occasions such as weddings and funerals, Jared would emerge to mingle with "normal" people for a few hours.

And when its over, we straight folk would be relieved when people like Jared returned to their gay ghettoes. And thankfully, we would survive potential embarrassment until the next family event.

Although it's hypothetical, I have outlined a depressing scenario. Outcome one is a violation of Jared's character and identity. It is also a sad reflection of my emotionally bankrupt state and callous disrespect for who he is.

It represents, however, attitudes that do exist in our communities. I need to understand how ultimately destructive denial and self-deception can be. I can't pretend to be a victim of circumstance (bad luck, I have a gay son) and use it as an excuse for not engaging fully with who he is.

I need to remind myself how seeds of denial, collusion and self-deception can take root and emerge, years later, as a subtle but pervasive doctrine of discrimination against the LGTBQ community.

If I tried to force or coerce Jared to be "less of a homo" and urged him to "behave more like a man," no amount of rewards, coercion or threats would have worked.

As a parent, I can't exercise any legitimate power over him to make him deny who he is or persuade him give up his orientation as a gay person. Under pressure from me and others, he could try and suppress who he is, to avoid being discriminated against. But the harm it would cause to Jared would be unconscionable on my part.

Outcome two, the route I took, has made me come face to face with my own assumptions and beliefs. Our conversations have opened me up to a new self-awareness of my fears, failures and frail humanity.

More significantly, though, it has also exposed me to the potential for my relationship with Jared.

The first time I came out for Jared, I was wallowing in a hot tub in Nova Scotia with three male friends on a snowy night in January. Our conversation had moved from customary guy talk to deeper things of the heart.

I was able to tell my friends that Jared was gay, albeit with some trepidation, because I wasn't sure how they would react. Because of their empathic understanding, my coming out as a parent has become easier each time.

For the foreseeable future it seems right that I come out for Jared and stand up for his uniqueness. One's sexual orientation will always be important, like one's religion. I hope that one day I will not need to come out for him anymore, because coming out will no longer carry the risk of rejection.

Every time I come out for him, I am also coming out for myself. Even though I am straight, by standing up for my son, I reinforce the notion that being gay is okay with me.

And being a parent of a gay person is absolutely and unreservedly a privilege.

A Complicated Love

~Chapter 11~
Coming out from religion

After my road trip with Jared, I started to think about the impact that imposed or unquestioned "truth" imparted by parents, caregivers and religious leaders can have on one's mind.

Not until I stepped back and looked at my beliefs more objectively did I realize the extent to which my own religion had influenced my approach to many issues, including my unquestioned rejection of homosexuality.

A case in point was my reaction when I first heard that Jared, my son, was gay.

As a minister, I used to interpret issues simplistically from a binary point of view — things were always black or white, good or evil. Was it God or Satan? Or, were they angels or demons?

I am reminded of the conversation I had with Jared on our road trip about an ultra-conservative U.S. radio host. Her style reminds me of how convinced I was that my viewpoint was God's viewpoint.

Those days it was common practice for me to search out and take pleasure in biblical verses that supported any position I held. On reflection, I think I chose a brand of Christianity that reinforced my view of the world, how I thought it should be, rather than as I have come to understand it really is.

Hiding behind a judgmental biblical text meant that I never had to engage authentically and listen in order to understand another person — I already had the answer, or so I thought.

Same-sex orientation was never debated amongst my colleagues, all of them males, because we all shared a common interpretation of the bible and a belief — homosexuality was a sin. Period.

We had no idea of the harm we caused because of our ignorance — our assumptions that people supress their heterosexuality and decide to be attracted to someone of the same sex.

As colleagues, we never discussed our own personal challenges with controversial issues such as homosexuality, masturbation, adultery and lust.

Maybe this was because we were all cut from the same cloth, in the sense that we grew up in a culture where men never gave themselves permission to discuss their own problems and how to arrive at an acceptable contextual understanding of these "sins" in society.

When issues like masturbation or homosexuality came up, I, like most of my colleagues, adopted an assumed condemnation without really exploring the historical biblical context, current research and physiological factors that probably would have made my opinions more relevant and would have given me much-needed insight.

How did my beliefs and role as a minister affect Jared when he was younger? And not only Jared, all my boys.

During the 1970's in South Africa, my mindset was pretty much shaped by a theological degree and years of claustrophobic Bible studies, seminars and sermons that were devoid of intellectual and scientific rigour.

After seventeen years of being in the ministry, it began to dawn on me that what I believed was only relevant within the confines of a religious paradigm.

Outside of that framework I felt irrelevant, because my language and conditioned responses had no meaning for those who did not subscribe to, believe in or understand the rules of the religious rituals I and others performed.

Towards the end of those years, I felt my words had a hollow ring, as if I were listening to but not believing in what I said.

It worried me that the God I believed in never seemed to manifest herself outside of the protective cloak of religious meetings. I began to ask if the faith I had followed was all smoke and mirrors and a figment of my own imagination.

Unbeknownst to my colleagues, I began to withdraw. I became an alien in the midst of a religion that had given me much comfort a few years before. I could no longer give comfort to a grieving mother whose daughter had died of incurable cancer.

I could no longer say I believed God was in control or a particular outcome was God's will.

I could no longer pretend I had insight into the will of God.

I was not sure that the One I prayed to actually cared or even existed.

I realized that for me, the divine moment had possibly moved on.

I had been steeped in religion. And I had questions. Big questions. Most of them were buried under the frenzy of activities that went with the job of being a disciple caught up in evangelical fervour.

To be true to myself, I could no longer perform rituals in the hope of evoking the divine. I needed to find myself again and learn a new language that had meaning for me.

~::~

Ten years later.

I am an avid photographer and most weekends over the last few years I have explored the backroads along the Fraser Valley, from just outside Vancouver to the town of Hope.

One of the institutions I drive past on these excursions is Trinity Western University (TWU), well-known for its covenant of exclusion that is held sacred by the university.

Recently I looked up the covenant and found the following excerpt which describes TWU's commitment to healthy sexuality and living a pure life:

"...according to the Bible, sexual intimacy is reserved for marriage between one man and one woman, and within that marriage bond it is God's intention that it be enjoyed as a means for marital intimacy and procreation."

If their covenant advocated celibacy amongst committed couples, we might respect the university's outdated but heartfelt call for students to commit to living a "righteous" life while studying.

But it specifically excludes same-sex couples. Their covenant implies that same-sex orientation is not Biblical, is unhealthy and sinful. Their covenant infers that same-sex couples have made a choice to follow a non-Biblical moral code, as opposed to Christian heterosexual couples who follow a biblical moral code and a righteous calling.

This is a fairly common religious belief. But each time I drive by, I get to thinking how TWU manages to reconcile its discriminatory religious covenant based on skunk science about same-sex orientation with its obligations to teach scientific methods of inquiry with integrity.

I wonder how an institution that prides itself on its academic record can espouse the pursuit of 'rigorous academic scholarship' and at the same time nurture a belief system about gay people based on Biblical scriptures taken out of context.

Simply put — what TWU is really saying is, "We will pursue rigorous academic scholarship in every field except for sexual orientation because the science contradicts our beliefs based on our interpretation of the Bible."

This for me is a good example of fundamentalism. James Hollis, a Jungian analyst and author, says that fundamentalism is, "an anxiety management system that finesses the nuances of doubt and ambiguity through rigid and simplistic belief systems."

We are, after all, living in the 21st century. We rely on scientific enquiry like no other time before.

This contradiction is not limited to TWU however. I see it across a broad sweep of institutions, churches and communities in North America and beyond, who ignore or avoid any research on same-sex relationships and harbour what I feel are simplistic religious beliefs about fellow human beings.

Seth Godin, a best-selling author and thought leader, says that a fundamentalist is "someone who considers whether a fact is acceptable to his religion before he explores it."

This is what I call the 'lead and lag factor' at the interface between the Bible and the dynamic evolving global society that we live in. Although the Bible and other holy books have enjoyed constant appeal, they remain static.

We can expect no new revelation to deal with the multitude of social and scientific issues facing modern societies.

Meanwhile, society is constantly evolving. Developments in science, technology and the humanities challenge our understanding of the universe and our place in it.

Nobody would argue that human society is transforming and adapting constantly – it would be as unrecognisable today to those who lived in recent history as it will be to ourselves in a hundred years time.

We accept new ethical norms, which eventually become accepted by society and even codified into law in some countries. In this sense society leads, and the Bible and other holy texts lag.

I am mindful that in 1632, Galileo was found guilty at a papal trial and put under house arrest for advocating a Copernican theory of the universe. Galileo believed that the earth circled the sun, which was contrary to the interpretation of scripture at the time.

Although the Bible is revered by millions as a complete revelation designed to meet all one's needs for guidance and inspiration, many still interpret the Bible with the same mindset as those who condemned Galileo nearly 400 years ago.

When St. Paul, one of the most prolific authors of the New Testament, assumed that everyone was born straight, we need to acknowledge that he wrote in all sincerity, yet with a pre-scientific world view.

Because he was not able to benefit from modern psychological insight, his revelation, however profound in many areas, was nevertheless influenced by his own culture, education and zeitgeist.

A case in point is the relatively recent development of human rights, which is now universally accepted as a moral good.

It is not yet 200 years since the abolishment of the Atlantic slave trade and slavery is explicitly outlawed in most countries.

And yet, if we return to the Bible, slavery is an example of oppressive domination. Slaves in the New Testament were expected to be obedient to their masters in all things, and were often severely punished for misdemeanours.

Sadly, there is no record of moral outrage and no proclamation that it was a "sin" to own the life of a fellow human being. The world-view of those prophets, disciples and sages was influenced by the homeostasis of the culture of the time – a binary world of sin or righteousness, devil or God, heaven or hell and good versus evil.

For example, a person suffering from epilepsy – what we now know to be a neurological disease characterized by seizures – would be diagnosed with demonic possession. All that was needed was an anticonvulsant medication in the form of an oral syrup.

Today society has, albeit slowly, acted on new insights about slavery and homosexuality.

Until recently, for example, plantation owners in the southern United States and other areas used the Bible to justify their practice of owning slaves.

And here's the point. If you accept that slavery violates human rights, and you acknowledge that you cannot use the Bible to justify the practice of slavery today, yet you attempt to draw on scripture written in the same historical context to condemn homosexuality, you apply a double standard.

The absence of outspoken critique by New Testament authors against sexism, patriarchy and violations of human dignity such as slavery, reminds us that although the authors had insight into the divine, their religious beliefs were tempered by the culture and socially accepted norms of their times.

The few verses that appear to directly condemn homosexuality are also a product of the same culture: They had no "divine insight" into the impact of chemicals in the brain such as testosterone or estrogen, for example, or the role of epigenetics — the way heritable traits are modified by environmental influences without changing our DNA.

Fortunately, slavery is not tolerated by most societies anymore because of laws that provide dignity and equality to all. And outside of the main religions, homosexuality is viewed with greater acceptance and understanding because of scientific research into same-sex orientation.

Despite emerging scientific views and a greater acceptance of same-sex orientation, the recognition of equal rights for gays is still inconsistent and slow in many of these same democracies.

Much of this can be attributed to the power of entrenched and unexamined religious beliefs.

~::~

Entrenched and unexamined religious beliefs

After the 2016 massacre in Orlando, for example, in which 49 people were killed in a gay nightclub, one minister said, "The tragedy is that more of them didn't die."

What an appalling response.

Willful ignorance and discrimination against people who have a same-sex orientation is a sickness of the heart and mind.

This corrosive belief and skunk science about same-sex orientation continues to this day – as evidenced by the comments of the minister, above.

While perpetuating myths and superstitions about people who have a same-sex orientation, some try to apply remedies such as prayer or conversion therapy in attempts to rectify what they perceive as a "fallen" or "sinful" lifestyle.

How do we find common ground with millions of Christians whose beliefs are based on what I would call myth and superstition?

Many beliefs extracted from the Bible and other holy books—the creation myth, Noah's ark and the flood, demons, devils and others—are not true, applicable or relevant today.

Quoting from scriptures or pointing to nature cannot be used to negate the biological normality of same-sex orientation in a civilised and scientific era.
Willful religious ignorance is a form of harm because it demeans human beings and reduces the complexity of sexual orientation to a black or white decision, a sin or righteous paradigm.

I am reminded of Leonard Cohen's Anthem, "Ring the bells that still can ring, Forget your perfect offering, There is a crack, a crack in everything, That's how the light gets in."

Many of these religious practitioners would experience a crisis of faith if they discovered a "crack in everything" they held sacred, especially the Bible.

Ironically, if they do go so far as to acknowledge that certain pre-scientific scriptures in the Bible are not applicable today, or the Bible contains errors, it would ignite a deep insecurity within them to discover a crack in everything they hold sacred.

LGBTQ people discover their sexual orientation over time. They eventually make a decision to come out to follow their innate orientation, often in an environment of religious ignorance and superstition.

There is no moral trespass, no sin.

Religion and superstition

Although there are exceptions, many historic church movements continue to become irrelevant in the modern world.

Their rituals, sacred dramas, myths and symbolism are still largely the only window through which the faithful interpret their world, often ignoring pressing social issues outside the walls of their institutions.

As these practitioners take comfort and pleasure in their religious texts and rituals, the world passes them by.

For example, a document on homosexuality released in 2005 by the Vatican circumvents use of the words sexual "orientation." Although sympathetic to individuals who have deep-seated homosexual "tendencies," the document fails to address the issue of sexual orientation and modern research.

Instead, it falls back on a view of sexuality and natural law rooted in Plato's teachings.

The document states, "Sacred Scripture presents them (i.e., homosexual tendencies) as grave sins.

The Tradition has constantly considered them as intrinsically immoral and contrary to the natural law. Consequently, under no circumstance can they be approved."

Sadly, the light filtering through the windows of the Catholic church and many other traditional Christian denominations and fundamentalist religious groups seems too dim to brighten the lives of same-sex couples who are not "immoral" and are not committing "grave sins" simply because of who they are.

The superstitious beliefs about gays within the Catholic church ignore modern research and cause untold harm to devout individuals who seek a home and acceptance in the house of God.

When I think about the people I used to work with in the church years ago, some are still held captive by similar narrow and robotic-like points of view — assuming that the "truth" resides in their interpretation of the scriptures or religion.

A growing trend in North America is the activism of conservative people who support laws that discriminate against the LGBTQ community because they believe that religious rights (making a stand against "perversion" and "evil") trump other civil rights.

By appealing to divine sanction, religious groups — in a type of twisted bigotry — expect to enjoy special civil rights, privileges and legal protections while denying the same rights to gays.

All self-righteous grandstanding about religious freedom that denies gay people respect, acceptance and social services is a 21st century evil built on the foundations of ignorance and superstition.

Religious freedom in some jurisdictions can mean that citizens have the right to their religious beliefs, even though some of their beliefs could be harmful and discriminatory to gays.

But religious freedom does not give anyone permission to discriminate against or deny service to the LGBTQ community.

In the US for example, a Colorado appeals court ruled recently that a Denver-area baker cannot refuse to make a wedding cake for a gay couple based on his religious belief.

I believe it's dishonest and cowardly to manipulate or quote religious texts out of context. Or to disguise discrimination as a moral return to family values. Or to use religious beliefs, superstition or tradition as an excuse to not have authentic dialogue with a son or daughter, or a colleague who happens to be gay.

Thankfully, I know sincere, religious people who are open and welcoming to the LGBTQ community. They radiate acceptance and love and don't feel compromised nor insecure in the expression of their faith.

Reparative and conversion theories of the religious right

Dr. Elizabeth Moberly, a British conservative Christian theologian who popularized reparative therapy within a religious context, believes that homosexuality is caused when a young boy lacks a positive relationship with his father.

She theorizes in her book, *Homosexuality: A New Christian Ethic*, that a boy would redirect his longing for a meaningful relationship with his father to other males in a search for connection and love.

The religious right feel that the same-sex orientation of a gay person can be changed with counselling and prayer. Many practitioners believe that by submitting to reparative conversion therapy, LBGTQ people can "revert" to a heterosexual orientation.

The National Association for Research & Therapy of Homosexuality (NARTH), also known as the NARTH Institute, is an organization that offers conversion therapy and other regimens that purport to change the sexual orientation of people with same-sex attraction.

NARTH and other groups such as Exodus, also believe people are born with a heterosexual orientation. Homosexuality, in their view, is a description of a condition and not a description of the intrinsic nature of the person. NARTH advocates believe that they are a service to help people who "experience unwanted homosexual attractions" and this can change with therapy.

A positioning statement on their website says:
Implicit in NARTH's view of homosexuality is the assumption that the nuclear family is the moral vanguard against homosexuality. Although they acknowledge prenatal hormonal influences, NARTH also views homosexuality as a possible result of incompetent parenting, sexual experimentation or sexual abuse.

It is worth pointing out that if inadequate or non-existent fathering is a factor in sexual orientation, we would have seen a dramatic increase in homosexual orientation during World Wars I and II when many fathers were sent off to the battle front.

What scientists are saying about conversion therapy

Few, if any, peer-reviewed scientific studies on the results of reparative or conversion therapy have been published. Therefore, no reliable scientific data is available for scientists to review post-therapy results. The only evidence available is anecdotal, mainly from 'ex-gays' and therapists themselves.

Doug Haldeman, a Counselling Psychologist in Seattle, Washington, believes sexual orientation conversion therapy is pseudo-science.

He wrote in the *Policy Journal of the Institute for Gay and Lesbian Strategic Studies* that, "This discredited and ineffective psychological treatment harms people and reinforces the notion that homosexuality is bad. In this regard, it is not a compassionate effort to help homosexuals in pain, but a means of exploiting unhappy people and of reinforcing social hostility to homosexuality."

Brian Mustanski, a psychologist at the University of Illinois at Chicago's Department of Psychiatry says one needs to consider the following three criteria when evaluating scientific research.

First, the public needs to know what authority and expertise the author has. He says, "Articles published in academic journals need to be reviewed by several qualified scientists before they are published."

Secondly, their research needs to be objective. He asks, "Is bias or opinion expressed when a writer interprets the research?" And finally, he comments on the accuracy of a report or scientific paper: "Is it peer-reviewed? Have the findings been replicated? Other scientists should be finding similar results."

Mustanski's three criteria — the authority and expertise of the author, the importance of a robust peer review process and the accuracy and replication of results — are critical.

These criteria are a buffer against the myth and superstition of pseudo-science proponents.

Scientists say sexual orientation conversion therapy is harmful, ineffective and potentially dangerous — in some cases it can trigger suicide. Conversion therapies or reparative therapies have no scientific basis and remain unproven forms of experimental therapy.

Many have observed that after 'therapy', the subjects that were cloistered within a religious community remained homosexual, albeit celibate homosexuals.

Doug Haldeman concurs: "There have been thousands of such individuals in my practice, and although they have experienced differential kinds of reactions, to a person they have been motivated by a religious terror that encompasses a variety of fears, including outright ostracization by their families and communities of faith.

The failure to succeed in conversion therapy is for many, doubly stigmatizing, and sometimes results in depression and suicidality, intimacy avoidance and sexual dysfunction, a highly prejudiced and negatively distorted view of LGBT people and our community, and a sense of 'de-masculinization', or failure to conform to the accepted norm of what a man 'should be'.

Sexual orientation and religious identification are both complex, deeply felt constructs that defy superficial or unproven treatments."

Christian counsellors and ministers who continue to use reparative and conversion therapy despite the research that it is harmful, ineffective and potentially dangerous are blind practitioners of immeasurable harm and out of step with 21st century science.
In my experience, gay people who are active members of their churches, mosques or synagogues receive lots of love within the community.

However, in the more fundamentalist churches, a gay person is slowly "guilted" over time and edged towards accepting they have a "condition" that is "unnatural" and can be rectified with prayer and therapy.

These sincere gay people want to do what is "right" and please God, their family and friends. They eventually submit to the type of "counseling" and "therapy" that NARTH advocates.

This is the moment when the blunt instruments of religious ignorance do immense harm — convincing a guilt-ridden person that their "decision" to have a same-sex orientation is against God.

Unfortunately, simplistic and unsophisticated approaches by sincere religious practitioners to the complexity of sexual orientation does untold harm to the psychological health and well-being of gay people.

As long as gay people are active within their religious communities and play an active role at the multitude of services, prayer meetings and bible-studies, they can — for a limited time — go through the motions and maintain their "straight" status with the support of the group.

But such a commitment comes at a great cost. My experience as a minister is that sooner or later the natural and innate urges of their same-sex orientation will surface through the veneer of religious compliance.

What many people in those religious communities don't see or experience is the devastating behind-the-scenes impact of depression and suicide as gay people wrestle with their feelings, their identity and their sense of humanity and try to reconcile these with the weight of religious guilt.

Put simply, no amount of prayer or therapy can change the innate sexual orientation of another human being.

Religious beliefs—like that of TWU and thousands of others—that discriminate against people with a same-sex orientation are rooted in the mysticism, myth and superstition of cultures that existed many thousands of years ago.

Rather than succumb to these primitive beliefs, we reveal our higher nature and empathic and civilized humanity when we embrace information based on science and engage with real people who just happen to have a same-sex orientation.

Given what we now know about sexual orientation, the problem with quoting religious texts that condemn same-sex relationships is that it is an unethical, irrelevant and harmful practice.

A same-sex orientation is most probably a complex interaction of genetic, hormonal, environmental, psychological and social factors.

It is not a choice.

I'd much rather have a real relationship with my son than follow a religion that forces me to compromise my unconditional love for Jared by adhering to religious dogma that ignores the latest research on same-sex attraction.

Here's the dilemma — love Jared as my son but reject his lifestyle of "'sin." But if Jared's sexuality is not a conscious choice, how can I expect him to suppress his sexuality and a part of his identity?

If he chooses to come out and be in a committed, loving relationship with his partner, living the lifestyle of his choice, what grounds do I have to judge him?

In coming to terms with Jared's homosexuality, I realised there was no "sin" or moral trespass on his part.

He never made a choice to have a same-sex orientation. He discovered it over time. He is a wonderful human being who happens to have a same-sex orientation.

But I faced a choice. I could follow my religion to the letter and reject Jared, or come out from my religion and embrace my son.

A Complicated Love

~Chapter 12~
Coming out authentically

W hen I face a personal challenge or a tough conversation lies ahead, two voices compete for my attention.

My autocratic voice wants to keep the status quo, to not investigate my assumptions or reconsider my way of doing things. My autocratic voice wants me to play it safe and to stick with the program by following and not challenging (religious) rules in my head that have been there for a long time.

My autocratic voice says it's a sign of vulnerability and weakness to show and express my emotions.

My authentic voice, on the other hand, calls for growth and discovery, challenging me to continuous learning, to build meaningful diverse relationships, to try new things and to break with rituals and beliefs that are no longer true for me.

My authentic voice says it's a sign of coherence and strength to show and express my emotions.

My autocratic voice urges me to embrace homogeneity, reject criticism and defend what I believe is right (it's in the Bible, after all), to not show weakness by disclosing what's really going on . . . ever.

My authentic voice urges me to avoid impression-management and the security of using my autocratic voice. If I succumb to the pull of my autocratic voice, fearing self-disclosure, I will not experience the power of meaningful dialogue with Jared and others.

The voice urges me to disable my autocratic voice and follow my heart. Only then, says the voice, will I flourish emotionally and connect with others, including Jared.

The two voices in my head—my autocratic voice—fearing the pain of self-disclosure, competes with my authentic voice—wanting to release the energy of real dialogue, the sensing and responding from my heart.

For years, instead of examining my internal voices, I insulated myself from being fully human and engaging with others, especially my sons.

It seemed a safe approach to not get involved. My emotional alienation was the path of least resistance, to the fragile peace of numbed-out testosterone.

My limited articulation of my emotions reinforced the image of myself as a stoic, an emotionally stunted clone of a cowboy movie hero who said no more than five words during the whole movie.

Since those road trip conversations—learning to use my authentic voice—I've been rewarded with a richer tapestry of experiences. And giving myself permission to articulate those experiences and emotions has allowed me to feel more human and more engaged.

As I begin to understand Jared's journey towards self-acceptance and wholeness, I've had to give up on any notion that I possessed insight into Jared's same-sex orientation.

When I reach into his experience, it empowers me to come out to others and articulate what I have learnt.

Although my love for him has never been in question, I can now say to Jared, "I accept you just as you are," and mean it.

A Complicated Love

~Chapter 13~

Closure

Hello Dad,

I finished the book on Tuesday and have been mulling over what to say. I think it is absolutely incredible.

Of course, the way I show up in the book is interesting. I generally still agree with what you say, though today I would add some nuances to some things I said and better explain my view in others.

But generally, I think the quoted lines are a very fair reflection of what I said and who I was at the time. That was five years ago.

It was also really compelling to read what you were thinking about and how you interpreted my comments and behaviour at the time, and how wary you were.

There is a disconnect there, which we could explore sometime over a bottle of wine. It goes to show that both of us made some big assumptions and the only way to know what somebody else is thinking is to ask them.

Most of all I liked the two last chapters. Your writing about your old style of communication resonates strongly with me.

It's what I have been talking about in therapy, and it is affirming for me in its truth.

Your comments on authentic communication, on embracing emotions and weaknesses, on hearing and accepting people, is also inspiring and true.

It is in part what I needed to hear from you, and in that sense is releasing for me.

I also appreciate your public support for me and my sexuality. In this you are extraordinary. I hope many people will read it and learn from your example.

Thank you for writing this book, I love you very much.
Jared

When I read Jared's e-mail, I felt both pain and relief as a tide of emotions surfaced through a stream of tears.

I immediately e-mailed Jared, who is now a school teacher and living on a narrow boat on the River Cam in Cambridge, England.

Hey Jared
Thanks for your most beautiful letter. You made me cry.
I love you too.
Dad

After reading Jared's e-mail, I felt an urge to connect with Jared again, face to face, father and son.

I booked a flight from Vancouver to the UK and spent two weeks in August hanging out with Jared on his boat. We spent many pleasant days renovating his boat and touring Cambridge's many historic colleges.

We had meaningful conversations over bottles of wine and Guinness.

One night Jared opened a box of photographs and showed me pictures of his school years that were especially telling and reflective of the challenges he was facing at the time.

We discussed the experiences he was going through, the influence of his mother on him, and the emotional distance between Jared and I at the time.

I apologised for not being there for him when he needed me the most. In that moment I felt a deep connection with Jared that I had never sensed before. We both experienced a profound release.

During the long flight back to Vancouver, I reflected on our journey together. What began for me as a complicated love is no longer the case.

I have become clear. I have changed.

My love for Jared has transformed from a complicated love to a committed love.

I encourage you to question your own assumptions about others and risk having authentic conversations. Yes, it will feel uncomfortable at first, and you will emerge knowing yourself, and others, more profoundly.

~Chapter 14~
Sexual orientation is complex

Traditionalists believe a large percentage of young children will become homosexual because they have been brought up or raised by parents who are gay or lesbian.

Common myths and taboos

They also say that same sex marriages or civil unions threaten the stability of the regular family and will eventually destabilize society. In their minds, an acceptance of homosexuality would lower standards, erode family values and weaken civil society.

Taboos tend to stick around because they are rooted deep below the topsoil of the conscious mind. David Bergman, a writer and English professor at Towson University, recognized this when he wrote, "Homosexuality is the last great taboo of American society."

The mere mention of same-sex relationships or homosexuality in some circles can trigger a knee-jerk reaction.

And when swept along on a rising tide of emotion, assumptions and beliefs about homosexuality can surface in a flash.

The idea that homosexuality is a psychological disorder or perversion, has its roots in the European sexologist movement that developed during the late 19th century.

Because homosexuals were classified as mentally ill, great injustices occurred over the years against homosexuals, as therapists attempted to cure them from their 'psychological disorder.'

Today, variations of earlier theories are still embraced and followed by therapists and counsellors who identify with a traditional and conservative approach to dealing with homosexuality.

Most traditionalists still believe homosexuality is a chosen lifestyle. Others believe that it is the result of poor parenting or sexual molestation or drug addiction.

The US armed forces have made concessions in their approach to homosexuality. The reality, however, remains that taboos exist despite the Pentagon's *Policy Guidelines on Homosexuality*.

Gays still have to be extremely vigilant to avoid harassment. Discrimination is blatantly rooted in the policy because it prohibits anyone who has sexual bodily contact with a person of the same sex from serving in the US military.

While gays are expected to repress their orientation, homophobes have a different set of rules and are not under the same 'don't ask, don't tell' type of scrutiny.

Exposing taboos — the European Court of Human Rights ruled against a policy of discrimination against homosexuals within the British Armed Forces. Until 2000, all known gay and lesbian soldiers were discharged.

Commanders felt soldiers with a same-sex orientation would "polarize relationships, induce ill-discipline, and as a consequence damage morale and unit effectiveness."

The British Armed Forces now has a policy of non-discrimination with zero tolerance for bullying or harassing a gay or lesbian soldier.

When one looks at common myths surrounding homosexuality and parenting, the American Psychological Association has it on record that there are no developmental differences in children with gay and straight parents with regard to their intelligence, popularity with friends, or psychological and social adjustment.

Secondly, the APA adds that there is also no evidence that homosexuals are more likely to molest their children compared to straight parents. And thirdly, gay parents are not a factor in determining the sexual orientation of their children.

In other words, contrary to traditional thinking, children brought up by same-sex parents grow up to be heterosexual.

Environmental factors

New research shows that elements in the environment of the parents of an unborn child – stress, drama, comfort, despair, sadness and so on — will have an impact on the child later on.

The neural network of the growing child will interpret the imprint of these elements when they occur and modify the behaviour of the genes to survive.

In his book, *The Biology of Belief*, Dr. Bruce Lipton, a stem cell biologist, says we can no longer use genes to explain why humans are at the top of the evolutionary ladder.

He points out that there is not much difference between the total number of genes found in many primitive organisms, animals and those found in humans.

He observes there is a type of fatalism in the field of gene research known as "gene myopia" that believes that our destiny is controlled by our genes alone.

A key point of his writing is to recognize that a gene is usually activated by a signal from the environment.

Lipton mentions that research conducted by Pray and Silverman show that environmental stress, emotions and nutrition can modify behaviour of the genes without changing their blueprint. And these changes can be handed down to future generations.

Parents act as genetic engineers, according to Lipton. The research of Surani, Reik, and Walter, suggests that a process of genomic imprinting has a profound influence on the mind and body of the child. In other words, what is going on in the lives of parents or caregivers can influence the quality of life of the newborn child.

Lipton points to studies showing that all children resonate with their mothers' feelings and emotions.

By way of illustration, if a mother is under stress, stress hormones are activated in the child's neural network via the umbilical cord and the bloodstream.

When these hormones pass through the placenta, the blood flow to the child can change and affect the child's nature:

"Eventually, the child is going to find itself in the same environment as its parents. Information acquired from the parents' perception of their environment transits the placenta and primes the prenate's physiology, preparing it to more effectively deal with future exigencies that will be encountered after birth. Nature is simply preparing that child to best survive in that environment."

So, according to Lipton and Pert, if a foetus is subjected to extreme fluctuations of emotions such as sadness, despair, worthlessness or contempt, the unborn child's psychosomatic neural network interprets, responds and adapts to this new reality in order to survive.

Further research is needed to explore the impact of emotional and environmental stressors on the psychological, emotional and sexual orientation of an unborn child.

Research on twins

Studies indicate that homosexual orientation can be detected very early in children. Childhood Gender Nonconformity, or CGN, is a behaviour that indicates an innate trait below the consciousness of the child.

The authors of *Sexual Orientation, Controversy, and Science* further define CGN, "More specifically, Childhood Gender Nonconformity comprises the following phenomena among boys: cross-dressing, desiring to have long hair, playing with dolls, disliking competitive sports and rough play, preferring girls as playmates, exhibiting elevated separation anxiety, and desiring to be—or believing that one is—a girl.

In girls, gender nonconformity comprises dressing like and playing with boys, showing interest in competitive sports and rough play, lacking interest in conventionally female toys such as dolls and makeup, and desiring to be a boy."

So, in theory, if an identical twin inherits a gene from the mother and that gene is switched off while his brother has the same gene switched on—and if that gene is somehow related to sexual attraction, it could explain why one twin would exhibit CGN and identify with a homosexual orientation and his brother would grow up with a heterosexual orientation.

Dr. Dean Harmer at the US National Cancer Institute is well known as the researcher who in 1993 announced that gay brothers shared a region of the X chromosome, known as Xq28.

Although other researchers have to date not been able to replicate his results, and many have been highly critical of his work, Dr. Harmer has said that much more research is necessary for us to get a better understanding of sexual orientation.

Dr. Brian Mustanski, Director of the Institute for Sexual and Gender Minority Health and Wellbeing in Chicago, concluded that although his team was unable to confirm the results of Dr. Harmer's discovery of the Xq28 region of the X chromosome as a cause of homosexuality, he found several DNA regions on three different chromosomes that could be linked to sexual orientation in males.

Mustanski observes that homosexuality tends to run in families. In a number of twin studies, the indications are that genes play a special role, especially in men. His studies show that identical twins have three identical chromosomes - numbers 7, 8 and 10.

His hypothesis is that identical chromosomes, together with hormonal influences, could play a role in their sexual orientation.

Psychologist Michael Bailey of Northwestern University and Psychiatrist Richard Pillard of Boston University also studied the sexual orientation of identical twins.

They found that if one twin is gay, the chances of the other developing a gay orientation is 52%. For fraternal twins, that number drops to 22%. The authors of *Sexual Orientation, Controversy, and Science* observe that, "We have reviewed evidence from twin studies showing that environmental influence on sexual orientation is considerable.

As we have tried to make clear, identical twin differences generally signal environmental influence, but the environment causing the differences need not comprise social influence.

That is, identical twins may differ in their sexual orientation not because of different social experiences but because of non-social differences, including those that took effect before they were born.

In other words, environment can be part of what is generally understood to be 'nature' rather than solely of 'nurture.' "

Testosterone and the male brain

Louis Berman, a professor of psychology at the University of Illinois at Chicago, now retired, makes the following comments with reference to his book, *The Puzzle: Exploring the Evolutionary Puzzle of Male Homosexuality*:

"Every person begins life with a proto-female brain. Testosterone masculinizes the brain (and genitals) of those embryos that are genetically marked to develop as males. Almost all male genitals are thoroughly masculinized. (There are rare exceptions.)

But, there is some direct evidence, and lots of indirect evidence, that there is a wide range of variation in the degree to which the male brain is masculinized. *The Puzzle* argues that the low-masculinized brain shades the inner life of the individual with female thoughts, feelings, and wishes.

This tendency, it is hypothesized, underlies gender-discordant behavior, fear of homosexuality, and homosexual behavior. As one unhappy homosexual man lamented, 'I am a male with a female brain.'

So the problem (for those for whom it is felt as a problem) or the fact of their homosexual situation begins with the fact that we all begin life as a proto-female, and that a few males end up with a low-masculinized brain.

What is the evidence that life begins for all of us as proto-females?

We all have nipples, that's the evidence.

As Leyner and Goldberg put it, 'During development, the embryo follows a female template until about six weeks, when the male sex chromosome kicks in for a male embryo.'

But before the end of the sixth week, a pair of sweat glands on the chest has already begun to differentiate as nipples. All infants are therefore born with nipples and some breast tissue.

As they approach puberty, the female hormones that course through the bloodstream of girls reshape their body in womanly ways, including the development of their breasts. Males are left with vestigial nipples, a reminder that life begins for all of us as proto-females, and some of us are fated to become more masculinized than others."

Neuroendocrinologist Günter Dörner, seems to concur. He postulates that the possibility of low levels of testosterone, or some way the brain of the unborn child responds to hormones, could cause sexual differentiation to proceed in a different way.

Wikipedia, the popular online encyclopedia, has a concise explanation of the way prenatal hormones can influence sexual orientation: "The neurobiology of the masculinisation of the brain is fairly well understood. Estradiol and testosterone, which are catalysed by the enzyme aromatase into dihydrotestosterone, act upon androgen receptors in the brain to masculinise it.

[The androgen receptor is an intracellular steroid receptor that specifically binds testosterone and dihydrotestosterone.]

If there are few androgen receptors (males with Androgen Insensitivity Syndrome) or too much androgen (females with Congenital Adrenal Hyperplasia) there can be physical and psychological effects.

It is likely that both male and female homosexuality is a result of a variation in this process."

Sexual orientation is complex

Timothy Murphy, a professor of philosophy at the University of Illinois College of Medicine says, "As a moral matter, homosexuality stands or falls only if it is compatible with key human values and social goods, not simply because it is biological.

That's the same test that applies to all sexual matters."

He also points out that "critics of homosexuality have it right when they worry that genetic studies undercut their authority."

An article from John Hopkins University's Faculty of Medicine on the subject of epigenetics and imprinted genes provides an additional perspective: "Genes carry the blueprints to make proteins in the cell. The DNA sequence of a gene is transcribed into RNA, which is then translated into the sequence of a protein.

Every cell in the body has the same genetic information; what makes cells, tissues and organs different is that different sets of genes are turned on or expressed."

Mustanski mentions the theory of the older brother, advanced by Dr Ray Blanchard, a researcher at the Centre for Addiction and Mental Health (CAMH) in Toronto.

If a mother produced anti-male antibodies, it could switch on or trigger a variant of a gene that would activate a homosexual orientation in the brain of the foetus.

Dr. Ray Blanchard also found that a younger brother's likelihood of becoming homosexual increased by about 33% for each brother that was born before him.

Mustanski concluded that although he had identified candidate genes within new chromosomal regions, there was no single gay gene, and that we should rather view sexual orientation as a complex phenomenon. His best guess is that differences in sexual orientation can be traced back to multiple genes either being switched 'on' or being moderated by environmental influences.

Robert Brookey, author of *Reinventing the Male Homosexual*, reminds us that we need to be aware of cultural influences and agendas that can distort research and to consider the downside of only looking for a biological cause for homosexuality.

"By identifying a biological cause for homosexuality, the gay gene discourse implies the possibility of correction."

And if there was a cure, it would imply that a same-sex orientation was a condition.

Would people like Elton John, Elizabeth Arden, Andy Warhol, Ann Bancroft, Lord Byron, Judy Garland, Rock Hudson, Johnny Mathis and millions of others, past and present, want to be "cured?"

Some gay rights activists hope that if sexual orientation is found to be hardwired, two things could change: biological research will help demystify homosexuality and usher in a better understanding of same-sex relationships and secondly, religious groups will lose the right to retreat to the smug comfort of divine authority and condemnation.

The Council for Responsible Genetics reminds us of the dangers of only looking for a biological fix for same-sex orientation: "The promise of a quick technological fix for the problem of discrimination against homosexuals distracts us from the larger societal issue.

Homophobia and discrimination exist, and it is naive to think that a biological explanation of homosexuality will change that. Only social and political remedies will counter discrimination."

The future

The struggle to end discrimination can be attributed to the work of activists like Martin Luther King Jr., Nelson Mandela and countless others who turned the tide against racism and made discrimination socially unacceptable.

Over the decades leaders such as Mahatma Gandhi, Mother Teresa, Bono and many LGBTQ activists have likewise awakened consciences in the quest for equality, justice, gay liberation, reduction of poverty and the eradication of AIDS.

The authors of *Sexual Orientation, Controversy, and Science* mention that, "The political rights of lesbian, gay, and bisexual (LGB) men and women have dramatically improved in many Western countries during the past 50 years."

Canada is the fourth country to legalize same-sex marriage by the passing of the Civil Marriage Act on the basis that equality and human rights are guaranteed in the Charter of Rights and Freedoms. An acceptance of traditional marriage to the exclusion of same-sex marriages would violate the Charter's guarantee of equality for all Canadians.

The Council for Responsible Genetics reminds us that, "The lesbian, gay, and bisexual community does not need to have its 'deviance' tolerated because its members were born 'that way' and 'cannot help it.' Rather, society must recognize the validity of lesbian and gay lifestyles. We need an end to discrimination, an acceptance of all human beings, and a celebration of diversity, whatever its origins."

The latest research has shown that there are hundreds of ways that genes work together and impact one another to change behaviour.

Nevertheless, we need to distance ourselves from research that says homosexuality is a biological error.
In the end, a biological argument, if ever proven, will most probably be insufficient to protect LBGTQ rights.

Can we conclude that homosexuality is the result of genetic determination and unknown environmental factors?

At best we can say there is insufficient evidence to conclude that a homosexual orientation is a result of nurture or nature alone. It is most probably a complex interaction of genetic, hormonal, environmental, psychological and social factors.

Daniel Goleman says the nature versus nurture debate is pointless and it's a fallacy to believe that genes and our environment are independent of each other. He says, "It's like arguing over which contributes more to the area of a rectangle, the length or the width."

As the movie, *Brokeback Mountain* so clearly portrays, when internalized sexual prejudice is deep-rooted in conservative communities, it can slowly ferment amongst homophobes into a compelling and pervasive doctrine.

Within a homophobic environment, gays and lesbians feel the pressure to deny part of their identity and conform to social constructs.

This can cause gays to hide in many communities, because they do not have sufficient legal protection and confidence in societal values to express their sexual orientation in public, or they fear for their personal safety.

On behalf of the American Psychological Association, Doug Haldeman honoured Diana Osanna, one of the producers of *Brokeback Mountain*.

The award is very clear about the costs of discrimination: "The film effectively and subtly illuminates the human cost of discrimination and outright bigotry that lesbian, gay, bisexual and transgendered people continue to face today. Its integrity and insight into the human experience of particular people in a particular time give *Brokeback Mountain* a rare power and resonance that we, as psychologists, salute."

Peter Tatchell, a gay and human rights activist, says we need to first go through the process of affirming that gays are different before we can usher in a more pluralistic culture where sexual difference is no longer a criteria for acceptance or non-acceptance. "This is the great paradox; only when sexual difference is fully accepted and valued will it cease to be important and slide into oblivion."

One of the best ways to break down walls is to be a deep listener. When we park all judgment and listen for what is meaningful and important to all of us, we discover our unique stories are all linked to the primal cry of the human heart — we are one.

A Complicated Love

About the Author

Dene Rossouw is a father of three sons.

He is the Principal Learning Facilitator at Team Possibil.com.

He lives on Vancouver Island and is an avid wildlife photographer.

A Complicated Love

CPSIA information can be obtained
at www.ICGtesting.com
Printed in the USA
BVHW070925310123
657444BV00004B/258